*Preserving the Chaldean Aramaic Language*

by Roy Gessford

San Diego, California
www.letinthelightpublishing.com

© 2020, Let in the Light Publishing

Library of Congress Control Number: 2020920461

ISBN# 978-0-9851125-6-1

Cover Art: Amy Grigoriou

Photo Credits:

Photographs are used with permission or are from the collection of Let in the Light Publishing. Additional photo credits include:

The photo on page 44 of my Hebrew teacher, Roni Rubinstein, is from an unidentified source.

Photo on page 50 of Queen Shammuramat, (Sammuramat) or Semiramis (Greek) and photo on page 54 of Cyrus Cylinder are from the British Museum.

Image of Iraqi region of Aramaic speakers on page 56 is from www.learningaramaic.blogspot.com.

Image of Galilean script on page 60 is from www.aramaicnt.org.

Image of Syriac script on page 60 is from www.biblescripture.net.

Image of Neo- Mandaic Aramaic script on page 61 and the image of Aramaic Square Script on page 62 are from www.omniglot.com.

**Preserving the Chaldean Aramaic Language**


A Capstone Action Project

Submitted to Claremont Lincoln University

in Partial Fulfillment of the Requirements for the

Masters of Interfaith Action

Roy Gessford

Claremont, CA

April 5, 2020

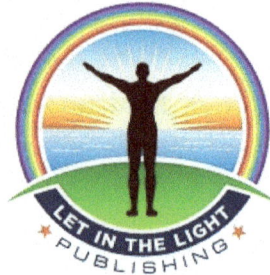

## Abstract

Aramaic, once a prominent language spoken by powerful ancient Near Eastern kingdoms, is now hovering near extinction. This capstone project tested the hypothesis that teaching an Aramaic class to an interfaith organization in San Diego, California, could serve as an effective method in preserving the Aramaic language. Twenty students from diverse backgrounds attended an hour-long interactive lecture on the history, relevance, and alphabet of the Aramaic language. Pre and post-surveys measuring interest and knowledge of Aramaic were administered. The increase in understanding of Aramaic was measured and recorded. My aspiration is that this project will inspire humanity to take an interest in preserving Aramaic. The preservation of Aramaic will be especially useful to future generations in understanding the deeper meaning of sacred religious and historical documents written in Aramaic and Semitic languages related to Aramaic such as Hebrew and Arabic.

*Keywords:* Assyrian, Chaldean, culture, Eastern Aramaic, interfaith, language, Neo-Aramaic, preservation, teach, workshop.

# Acknowledgements

I would like to thank God, Love, for guiding and guarding the ideas in this capstone project from start to finish. Divine Love's angels came in various forms. The team at Claremont Lincoln University (CLU) was exceptional. From the initial meeting with Dr. Darrell Ezell to the intriguing professors and students along the way, my heart is filled with gratitude. The expertise of CLU staff members Dr. Ashley Gimbal, Dr. Nosakhere Thomas, and Dr. Keith Burton was especially appreciated in the completion of this capstone.

The stakeholders assembled for this project constituted a remarkable group. Dr. Geoffrey Khan, Dr. Rocco Errico, Dr. Yona Sabar, Dr. Shin Kang, and my Aramaic professor, Fr. Michael Bazzi, were selfless in sharing their priceless wisdom. Rev. Karen Koblentz's unique ability to shepherd the San Dieguito Interfaith Ministerial Association (SDIMA) and organize a lecture on preserving Eastern Aramaic on less than three weeks' notice was greatly appreciated. The twenty participants in the class are the unsung heroes of this project. All had the courage to leave their comfort zones behind, and spend a Friday evening learning and sharing ideas on the precious Aramaic language.

Scholarships provided by CLU and grants from the Albert Baker Fund were incredibly helpful toward the completion of this project. I would like to thank my parents for their support. Finally, I would like to thank my Christian Science teacher, Bruce Fitzwater C.S.B., for his prayers, support, and consistency during the five-year process of completing this capstone project.

# Contents

## List of Tables

## List of Figures

## CHAPTER 1:  Introduction

**Preserving Aramaic**

Aramaic, one of the oldest spoken languages, is in danger of becoming a dead language (Khan, 2018; McWhorter, 2015; A. Sabar, 2013; Sabar 2018).  During the latter half of the first millennium B.C.E., Aramaic was the lingua franca (common language) of most of the Near East and the official language of the powerful Assyrian, Babylonian, and Persian empires (Sabar, 2018).  Aramaic was essentially the international language before such a thing existed (Sabar, 2018).  Chaldean Aramaic is a dialect of Eastern Aramaic and its roots predate ancient Babylon. The focus of this paper is how to sustain the precious Chaldean Aramaic language.

As an early Semitic language, Aramaic antedates Hebrew and Arabic.  Thus, preserving Aramaic is of interest to those whom sacred texts were written in Semitic languages or whose roots spawned from the Near East.  A. Sabar (2013) wrote that during its prime, Aramaic was spoken by Christians, Jews, Mandeans, Manicheans, Muslims, Samaritans, Zoroastrians and pagans.  Although all these groups have an interest in preserving Chaldean Aramaic, modern Chaldean Aramaic speakers have the greatest interest in preserving their dialect (M. Bazzi, personal communication, August 30, 2018).

**Social Significance**

Hanna-Fatuhi (2012) categorized Modern Chaldean Aramaic speakers into three groups of native Iraqis: Chaldeans, Syriacs (not to be confused with Syrians), and Atturaie or Assyrians. Hanna-Fatuhi (2012) wrote that the Chaldean-Syriacs descend from Abraham and are related to ancient celebrated kings, such as Sargon, Hammurabi, and Nebuchadnezzar II.  In modern times, all three groups of native Iraqis have faced tremendous persecution in Iraq, and this has resulted in a diaspora of native Iraqis.

The cost of losing Chaldean Aramaic is easier to measure qualitatively than quantitatively. A. Sabar (2013) noted that by the end of the century, fifty to ninety percent of the roughly 7,000 languages spoken today are expected to become extinct. Due to the unique history of the Aramaic language, its loss would stretch beyond the linguistic into cultural, religious, and historic significance. Literary epics from Gilgamesh to parts of the Hebrew books of Ezra and Nehemiah were written in Aramaic. Jesus and his disciples spoke Aramaic, the lingua franca of their day. When one realizes that the Hebrew of Jewish scripture and the Arabic of Islam have their roots in Chaldean Aramaic, one sees that Aramaic is woven into the very fabric of humanity (Testen, 1985).

**Personal Significance**

My own introduction to the existence of Aramaic came about in the following manner. After I had finished a course on biblical Hebrew in 2013 at the Graduate Theological Union in Berkeley, California, a friend emailed me a video of an Aramaic scholar, Dr. Rocco Errico. Intrigued by the video, I called Errico and inquired where I might learn Aramaic. Errico gave me the contact information of Fr. Michael Bazzi, a Chaldean Aramaic professor at Cuyamaca College in San Diego, California. Upon learning of my background in Hebrew, Fr. Bazzi invited me to join his intermediate modern Aramaic course taught the next semester.

After determining that this was a special opportunity, I moved to San Diego and enrolled in modern Aramaic in the spring of 2014 at Cuyamaca College in Rancho San Diego. Subsequently, I have taken Fr. Bazzi's Classical Aramaic course three times. Learning Aramaic has greatly enhanced my study of the Scriptures. Along with Hebrew, I have studied Greek and Latin languages. All my ancient language study has been helpful, but my study of Aramaic has brought the greatest insight into the life and teachings of Jesus.

My study of Aramaic expanded when Fr. Bazzi asked me to be his publisher. Since 2014, my company, Let in the Light Publishing, has published eight of Fr. Bazzi's books. These include six books on teaching modern and classical Chaldean Aramaic and two books on Chaldean and Iraqi history. Two of the books were co-authored by Dr. Rocco Errico. Working with these two Aramaic scholars on their books helped my understanding of the culture which Aramaic came from and the Aramaic language.

Due to the modern Iraqi diaspora, thousands of Chaldean Aramaic speakers now live in the United States, with San Diego and Detroit having the largest populations (Bacall, 2014). Most of my classmates at Cuyamaca College were natives of Iraq. In their homeland of Iraq, my classmates were prohibited, under the penalty of death, from learning their native tongue in a classroom setting. Many of these classmates were parents and grandparents trying to keep their native tongue alive. A. Sabar (2013) corroborated that in their new lands, few children and even fewer grandchildren learn Aramaic. A. Sabar (2013) predicted that this generational rupture marked a language's last days. Although daunting, the imperative to preserve Aramaic seems evident.

Part of my effort to preserve this language has been to teach Chaldean Aramaic. Following the teachings of Bazzi and Errico (2015), I have taught Chaldean Aramaic to a diverse group of inmates at the San Diego County Jail. This group included a gang leader from Louisiana, a retired Marine, a native Mandarin speaker, and a member of the Kumeyaay (San Diego) Native American tribe. Several inmates had been diagnosed with mental illnesses and learning disabilities. In addition, I have taught Chaldean Aramaic at several Christian Science churches, that included a student in her nineties. Although not an easy to language to learn, my experience suggests that anyone with a strong enough desire can learn the basics of Chaldean Aramaic.

## Conclusion

The specific method for preserving the Aramaic language in this capstone project will be to teach a Chaldean Aramaic class to the San Dieguito Interfaith Ministerial Association (SDIMA). It is hoped that by teaching an Aramaic course to members of an interfaith group, that they will share the information with their respective faith communities. This focused and thoughtful approach will introduce Chaldean Aramaic to those who genuinely desire to learn Aramaic. Although many other approaches to saving a language exist, given the specific requirements of this action research project, it may be wise to follow the adage that one cannot scatter his or her fire, and at the same time hit the mark (Eddy, 1875). Approaches by other scholars to save the Aramaic language include recording native Aramaic speakers, writing articles for academic journals, creating Aramaic instruction manuals, online education, and lecturing.

In Chapter 2, I will conduct a literature review. First, I will examine five sources relating to the theory of preserving languages. Next, I will synthesize twelve sources that relate to the practice of preserving Aramaic.

## CHAPTER 2: Literature Review

**Introduction**

The following literature review traces the history of Aramaic speakers from ancient Mesopotamia to modern day America. Aramaic, which was once spoken by kings, queens, pilgrims, and prophets, is on the verge of extinction. Aramaic stems from Akkadian, the language of the patriarch Abraham. The study of Aramaic is helpful in gaining a deeper understanding of other Semitic languages such as Hebrew and Arabic. The loss of Aramaic would limit the understanding of the followers of monotheistic faiths. This literature review begins with a review of the theory of language preservation and then documents the efforts of those trying to save Aramaic.

A note to the reader should be made that this literature review focused on preserving Aramaic in its earliest forms still existent from the Mesopotamia region. Terms for this older strain of Aramaic include some dialects of North-Eastern Neo Aramaic (NENA), Chaldean, Assyrian, Eastern Aramaic, and Neo-Aramaic. The family of dialects belonging to Western and Jewish Aramaic are more recent, and although still needing to be preserved, are not deemed as imminently necessary as the dialects directly linked to the Mesopotamia region.

The databases used for this literature review drew from databases available within the Claremont Lincoln University Library. Specific databases included Google Scholar, ERIC, JSTOR Open Access, and the Social Science Research Network. Terms searched for within these databases included, "preservation of language theory," "preservation of Aramaic language," "language revitalization," and "revitalization of Hebrew language." Articles on preservation theory dated back to 1987 and were obtained from scholarly journals. The literature reviewed which detailed modern attempts to save Aramaic drew from books as well as scholarly journals and dated from within the last ten years.

**Theory of Language Preservation**

Languages are disappearing at an alarming rate. Davis (2009) estimated that half of the languages of the world are teetering on the brink of extinction. Language revivalists placed struggling languages into two categories: the process of restoration, which aims at returning the language to a previously healthier state, and the process of transformation which seeks new roles for the language (Benthalia & Davies, 1993). Scholars noted that the only language to be restored is Hebrew (Nahir, 1988). Due to the similar loss of a homeland for native Aramaic speakers, the political history of the Chaldeans and other native Iraqis, and the importance of the Aramaic language for liturgical uses, my hope is that Aramaic can follow the path of Hebrew toward restoration. All other language revival efforts have taken the route of language transformation. An example of language transformation was when linguists attempted to preserve Gaeltacht, an Irish dialect. Preservation efforts emphasized youth education, and tactics such as singing contests for adolescents, language related sports teams for toddlers, and prizes for language-championing essays (Fishman, 1987). Although language transformation has been proved successful by scholars, language restoration for Aramaic, like Hebrew, began through the liturgy.

Cope and Penfield (2011) presented a collective viewpoint from seven scholars within the applied linguistics field pointing out that endangered language communities need to rely on training as well as teamwork and collaboration in order to survive. The authors emphasized that educational materials are needed to meet the pedagogical needs of endangered language communities. In addition, the authors maintained that training in applied linguistics empowered members of the speaking community, terminology needed to be examined, and linguistic skills needed to be adapted into nontraditional teaching concepts.

Golden (2001) presented an example of successful revitalization of the Hebrew language. A professor at Haifa University, Golden monitored a state-sponsored five-month, intensive Hebrew language class (ulpan) given to adult newcomers from the former Soviet Union. This ulpan featured eight students and a female teacher in her thirties. Through Hebrew instruction, the newcomer's Jewish Israeli national identity was formed. Golden (2001) showed that through Hebrew language study new social relationships and feelings emerged.

McWhorter (2015) wrote of the imminent demise of the Aramaic language. After chronicling the proud history of Aramaic as the lingua franca (common language) from Greece and Egypt, across Mesopotamia and Persia to India, from 600 to 200 B.C.E., McWhorter noted that Aramaic speakers have dwindled to less than 500,000 spread throughout the globe. McWhorter (2015) pointed to geographic fragmentation as one reason for Aramaic's demise. According to this fragmentation theory, Aramaic speakers spread themselves so widely across the globe that there was not a single "Aramaia" for speakers to rally behind (para 4). Instead, Aramaic varieties exist in obscure communities spread across Iran, Turkey, Iraq, Syria, Georgia, and Armenia, as well as expatriate communities in such locales as Chicago and New Jersey. This fragmentation has also led to the various names Aramaic goes by now such as Chaldean, Syriac, Assyrian, and Mandaic.

Suina (2004) reported on six Native Language Teachers (NLT) in New Mexico who are working to preserve the Pueblo language. After documenting the historic decline of the Pueblo language, exacerbated by the pressure to learn English, Suina (2004) recorded the recent attempt at language revival. Suina, who is himself Pueblo, undertook this study in 2002. The six teachers instructed four separate programs at both public and BIA (federally funded schools through the Office of Indian Education) schools. Suina (2004) traced the history and language background of each NLT and shared that a common theme among the NLT's was accountability to the tribal council and schools. NLT's faced pushback from parents who wanted their children to learn other subjects and a lack of time within the curriculum given to the subject. Suina (2004) did not use a metric as evidence of the success of the program, but concluded that preservation of culture, educating non-Native staff on Pueblo history, and changing attitudes will all assist in the preservation of the Pueblo language.

**History of Aramaic and its Speakers**

Aramaic has been vital to humanity for longer than any spoken language. Hanna-Fatuhi, (2012) wrote a comprehensive history chronicling the people of Mesopotamia, ranging from its earliest inhabitants over 100,000 years ago to what is now known as Iraq. Hanna-Fatuhi (2012) chronicled Chaldean kings from Sargon the Great (2334 - 2279 B.C.E.) to the first lawgiver, Hammurabi, (1792 - 1750 B.C.E.) to Nebuchadnezzar II (604 - 562 B.C.E.), who created the Hanging Gardens of Babylon for his homesick wife. Hanna-Fatuhi (2012) clarified that the first recorded queen of power, Queen Shummuramat/Shamiram, who ruled Assyria between 811-808 B.C.E., was originally a Chaldean princess. Hanna-Fatuhi (2012) traced the heritage of Chaldeans and their language through their ancestral heritage of Sumeria and Akkadia. The modern spoken Aramaic, Soureth, germinated from this early source.

Hanish (2009) gave a history of three Aramaic speaking tribes in Iraq: the Assyrian, Chaldean, and Syriac. The author recorded that at the beginning of the seventh century, about half the population was Christian. By the end of the eleventh century the population had become majority Muslim. Hanish (2009) highlighted that in the 1970's under the rule of Saddaam

Hussein, Chaldeans were prohibited from speaking Aramaic and forced to choose either Arab or Kurdish identity. Chaldean children were forced to study the Qur'an. Hanish (2009) noted that after Hussein's government fell in 2003, conditions worsened for Chaldean Christians, Yazidis, and Mandaeans. This included ethnic cleansing, rape, murder, church bombing, and kidnapping by the Islamic State. Hanish (2009) wrote that in Mosul, Christians were given the options to convert to Islam, pay a tax, or be beheaded. Many Christians chose the fourth option: flee. As of 2006, the Christian, Aramaic speaking population in Iraq had decreased from 1.2 million to 600,000 (Hanish, 2009). Since 2006, the Aramaic speaking population has continued to diminish.

**Loss of Aramaic Language Speakers**

Bazzi, (2015) monitored the drastic change that took place in his beloved hometown of Tilkepe in northern Iraq, about fifteen kilometers from Mosul. Up until the 1990's Tilkepe, which means hill of stones, was a prosperous village with over 10,000 residents. This author recounted the history of Tilkepe by sharing that Tilkepe first became populated in the 14th century when Timorling attacked nearby Mosul and the residents found refuge in Tilkepe. Bazzi (2015) noted that a 1968 census taken by Catholic priests showed 7,120 Chaldean Catholics, 551 Assyrian Catholics, and 600 Muslims. This author further shared that Tilkepe was the largest Christian village in the area from 1500-1900 A.D. and provided details about many cultural aspects of Tilkepe including information about boys' and girls' education, marriage, farming traditions, health care, architecture, and language. Bazzi (2015), a Chaldean Catholic priest currently residing in San Diego, California, noted that when he returned to Tilkepe in 1994, the spoken language of Aramaic (Soureth) had begun to diminish due to immigration. On a sad, final note, Bazzi (2015) wrote that by 2015, Tilkepe was a ghost town with all the doors of the homes of Christians marked with red paint by ISIS.

Coghill (2018) classified the language spoken by the Chaldean Catholic Christians of Tilkepe within the family of the North-Eastern Neo Aramaic (NENA) dialects. Coghill (2018) noted that the dialect of Tilkepe, located on the Mosul plain, is unique from the surrounding villages of Alqosh, Qaraqosh, and Batnaye and deserved a separate description. Coghill's (2018) paper focused on the phonology, morphology, and lexicon of the dialect and used a myriad of examples in her description of the sounds of consonants and vowels. Pronouns, nouns, adjectives, verbs, and copulas were covered in her explanation of morphology (Coghill, 2018). Coghill's (2018) lexicon sampled common and restricted words known to vary between NENA dialects.

**Chaldean Aramaic use in United States**

Two American cities, Detroit and San Diego, have become home to thousands of Chaldean Aramaic speakers. Bacall (2014) began his history of modern-day Chaldeans in Detroit with a general history of the Chaldeans and their religion and language. Bacall (2014) revisited the contributions of the Chaldeans over the millennia including the world's first empire which provided the setting for the literary epic of Gilgamesh and the construction of Babylon. Bacall (2014) wrote that the Chaldeans discovered the wheel, bronze weapons, horse-drawn carriages, as well as many other amenities common to cities and the disciple Thomas first brought Christianity to the Chaldeans. This author noted that the first converts to Christianity were Chaldean Jews. Bacall (2014) included a wonderful selection of photographs ranging from Gilgamesh to modern day Chaldeans in Detroit. This author further noted that Aramaic preceded Hebrew and Arabic, and that Classical Aramaic was still used in the church liturgy in Detroit.

Bazzi (2018), a Chaldean, wrote about Chaldean history and contributions to humanity and the current Iraqi diaspora. Bazzi (2018) noted that Chaldeans are from Mesopotamia – the land between the Tigris and Euphrates Rivers. From this region of the world, located in modern

Iraq, originated political, judicial, religious, and military systems that marked early civilization.

Mesopotamia also lays claim to the first form of writing, basic mathematical principles,

astronomy, and astrology among other contributions. Bazzi (2018) noted the significant spiritual

contribution of the Chaldeans and included a chart of all the times Chaldeans were mentioned in

the Bible. Bazzi (2018), a Catholic priest, recorded that Christianity had flourished among

Chaldeans and Assyrians in Mesopotamia since the second century and that since 1951,

Chaldeans have settled in San Diego, California. Bazzi (2018) provided an overview of the

Chaldean Catholic Church and noted that Chaldean Aramaic was used as its principal language,

including San Diego Chaldean Catholic churches.

**Modern Decline of the Aramaic Language**

Although media coverage of the Iraqi diaspora and loss of Aramaic is often not much

more than a sound bite, several scholars have been working to keep this struggle in the forefront.

Sabar (2018) shared his efforts to save his native Aramaic tongue. Sabar (2018) traced how

Aramaic had morphed over the centuries in a similar way as many other languages. A retired

UCLA professor, Sabar (2018), shared how he grew up speaking modern Aramaic, classified by

scholars as Neo-Aramaic, in his hometown of Zakho, Iraq. Sabar (2018) wrote about his Aliya

(immigration to Israel) and subsequent academic career in the United States. Recognized for his

contribution to the growing field of Jewish Neo-Aramaic, Sabar (2018), played a key role in

translating Jewish religious literature as well as translating oral traditions such as folktales,

personal anecdotes, folksongs, and proverbs. Sabar (2018) noted that the Iraqi diaspora is

greatly affecting the viability of Neo-Aramaic and poignantly wrote, "As a native speaker, I am

one of the last to possess some advantage in locating suitable [*sic*] native speakers" (p. 68).

A. Sabar (2013) recorded a day spent in the Chicago suburbs looking for native Aramaic speakers (informants) with University of Cambridge professor Geoffrey Khan. A. Sabar (2013) masterfully weaved the proud history of Aramaic and current decline into his article. A. Sabar (2013) described how Khan interviewed Agnes Nissan Esho, one of the last remaining speakers of her Aramaic dialect. With true Middle Eastern hospitality, Ms. Esho served an elaborate lunch while Professor Khan queried Ms. Esho for pronunciation of key words and phrases. Though a colorful and fun to read account, A. Sabar (2018) pointed out that many Aramaic dialects are already extinct and other dialects are down to a few remaining speakers.

**Efforts to Preserve the Aramaic Language**

A handful of dedicated scholars are working to document spoken and written dialects of Eastern Aramaic. Khan (2018), a scholar of North-Eastern Neo-Aramaic (NENA) dialects, started an audio library at Cambridge University to record native speakers before their dialect becomes extinct. Khan (2018) wrote that over 150 diverse dialects spoken by both Christians and Jews existed and that NENA dialects of Aramaic differ from the western dialect of Syriac (Aramaic) and the Jewish Babylonian Aramaic to the south. Khan (2018) delineated that within NENA there were fundamental splits in the linguistic structure and lexicon between Jews and Christians. This author noted that one subgroup of Christian dialects was the subgroup within the Mosul plain in Nineveh, Iraq. Khan (2018) noted that many NENA speakers from Central Iraq migrated north during the Middle Ages when the region had become largely Arabic speaking. This researcher registered that some Jewish dialects are already extinct and several of the Christian dialects are endangered. A pertinent point made by Khan (2018) was that the NENA dialects have strong oral tradition, but a systematic written way did not exist until the seventeenth century. This author also provided an analysis across NENA dialects.

Bazzi (2017) produced a primer of Modern Aramaic Chaldean Dialect. Bazzi (2017), an Aramaic professor, began his college-level textbook with a brief history of the Chaldeans and their origin in Mesopotamia, also known as "The Cradle of Civilization" (p.i). Bazzi (2017) introduced the twenty-two letters, eleven sounds, and seven vowels of the Chaldean Aramaic modern alphabet. Grammar rules for the language including alternative spellings, doubling, unpronounced letters, and occulted letters were covered. The basics of verbs and pronouns and a section on vocabulary that helped the student read, write, and speak Soureth were introduced. Bazzi (2017) included a section on Chaldean proverbs in Soureth and a folk song from the Iraqi city of Tilkepe. The book concluded with a written version of The Lord's Prayer in Soureth. Efforts are also being made to preserve older dialects of Eastern Aramaic. Bazzi and Errico, (2015) teamed together and wrote a college level textbook on Classical Aramaic. These authors date the Aramaic language in this book to the second century A.D. Bazzi and Errico (2015) introduced the Classical Aramaic alphabet and included the Estrangela letters which make written Classical Aramaic unique. In addition, the authors introduced general basic rules, nouns and adjectives, inseparable prepositions, pronouns, and verbs. The bulk of the vocabulary introduced has biblical signification. The authors (2015) concluded with the Lord's Prayer and the Beatitudes in Classical Aramaic.

Coghill (2009) presented four different versions of a children's story named, The Story of the Sparrow with a Thorn in His Foot. This story was orally passed down the generations and was recounted in the northern Iraqi villages of Alqosh, Tilkepe, and Hamziye, and the southern Iranian village of Tazakand. The origins of this bedtime story are unknown to the author nor is it known how the story travelled between the villages. Coghill (2009) observed variation from each location of the story. The premise of the story was that a sparrow got a thorn stuck in its foot, traded the thorn for bread, traded the bread for a ram, traded the ram for a bride and groom, and sang a song about its escapade. There are strong similarities between the versions of the stories told by the Iraqi villagers. The greatest variation occurs in the version of the story told from the Iranian villager. Coghill (2009) noted that the four dialects of Aramaic spoken by the storytellers are diverse, although there were similarities in literary devices.

**Conclusion**

In conclusion, Aramaic speakers have a unique history which is quickly being lost. Language preservation theory indicates that Hebrew was preserved for centuries through liturgical means and revitalized with the creation of modern-day Israel and Hebrew language immersion for newcomers. This model provides hope that Aramaic can be preserved through liturgical use and revitalized at some point. The bulk of Aramaic speakers have left their homeland, and the effort to preserve this language has become global. The Iraqi diaspora has placed Aramaic speakers on every continent except Antarctica. Through the efforts of dedicated scholars, teachers, families, and priests, it is hoped that a record of Aramaic will be preserved for future generations. The effort to preserve the Aramaic language by teaching is especially strong in San Diego, California.

In Chapter 3, I lay out the goals, methods, and measurements for this capstone project. After stating the research question, I will describe how I intend to teach an Aramaic workshop to an interfaith group in order to help preserve Eastern Aramaic. I will share the flier used to promote the event and introduce the pre and post-surveys which I intend to use for mixed methods of quantitative and qualitative measurement.

## CHAPTER 3: Research Plan

**Project Goal**

The trend toward the disappearance of the Aramaic language must be reversed in order for humanity to benefit from the treasures hidden within its usage. The loss of a homeland for native Aramaic speakers is tragic. Global efforts to preserve Aramaic must increase, especially in regions like San Diego, California, where the population of Aramaic-speaking refugees is significant. Although efforts have been made to publicize the demise of Aramaic, and even to record the final speakers of certain dialects, a consecrated effort to teach Aramaic to interested students needs to be made.

The reasons to preserve the Aramaic language are manifold. Aramaic's unique position as the oldest spoken language by humanity illustrates its historical significance. A form of Aramaic was spoken by Nebuchadnezzar, Jesus, and Jesus's disciples. As a Semitic language, Aramaic predates Hebrew and Arabic and is useful to understanding word origins for sacred texts written in those languages. Old Aramaic was the lingua franca under Assyrian, Chaldean, and Persian rule and Aramaic's use stretched the Near East. Finally, as the spoken language of the remaining Chaldean and Assyrian people, Neo-Aramaic remains a link to a culture that merits preserving.

An early idea for this Capstone Project suggested by the Dean of Capstone Studies, Dr. Stan Ward, was to record native Aramaic speakers and contribute to the archive started by Geoffrey Khan at Cambridge University. While this idea had merit and was considered, the idea to teach a workshop or class on Aramaic to an interfaith group was later suggested by the Chair of the Masters of Arts in Interfaith Action at Claremont Lincoln University, Dr. Keith Burton. The Aramaic workshop idea was better suited for interfaith work, and the research question, "To what extent is teaching an Aramaic language course to a San Diego, California, interfaith group effective in preserving the Aramaic language?" was adopted.

The preservation of Aramaic in San Diego will take a sustained, communal effort. Among others, Fr. Michael Bazzi has established himself as a central figure in the preservation of Aramaic in San Diego. Bazzi has been teaching modern and classical Aramaic at Cuyamaca College since 1989. Bazzi wrote or co-authored six books on teaching the Aramaic language. I will use Bazzi's *Read and Write Aramaic in Modern Chaldean Dialect* (*R&W*) as the foundation for teaching the course on Aramaic with San Diego Interfaith Ministerial Association (SDIMA).

In addition, I have engaged Bazzi as a stakeholder on this capstone project. Other individuals who have agreed to be stakeholders on this project are renowned Chaldean Aramaic scholar, founder of the Noohra Foundation, and co-author on two of Fr. Bazzi's books, Dr. Rocco Errico. Dr. Geoffrey Khan, who has started an audio library at Cambridge University, England, has also agreed to be a stakeholder. Dr. Yona Sabar, a native Aramaic speaker from Zakho, Iraq, and professor emeritus in UCLA's Near Eastern Languages and Cultures Program has agreed to be a stakeholder as well as Rev. Dr. Shin Kang, a retired Sumerian professor at Yale. SDIMA chair, Rev. Karen Koblentz, has agreed to be a stakeholder. Certainly, all the participants in the Aramaic workshop will be stakeholders as well.

**Project Methods**

The literature review brought forth the effectiveness that teaching a language course can have on saving a language. Golden (2001) detailed the progress which Hebrew has made as a spoken language, and that the Hebrew language is the only language to achieve full revival. To a lesser extent, Suina (2004) demonstrated the effectiveness that teaching can have in preserving a language in helping to save the Pueblo language.

The goal of teaching an Aramaic workshop to be given to SDIMA is to introduce participants to the Aramaic language and the challenges surrounding the language's longevity. Although modest in scope, the workshop has four learning outcomes. The first outcome is to expose participants to the history of Aramaic and the relevance Aramaic holds to sacred texts. The second learning outcome is to differentiate between the types of Aramaic dialects such as Eastern, Western, Mandaic, and Jewish Aramaic. The third learning objective is to understand the basics of the Chaldean Aramaic Alphabet. The fourth objective to is to share sustainability strategies for the Aramaic language.

The Aramaic workshop will be one hour in duration. A copy of *R&W* will be given to each participant. *R&W* contains the 22 consonants of the Aramaic-Chaldean Alphabet, the seven Aramaic vowels, the eleven sounds, and the six Estrangela letters which students in the workshop will find helpful in learning the basics of the alphabet. *R&W* also contains numbers, pronouns, verbs, grammar, and the Lord's Prayer, but those will not be covered in the initial workshop. Rev. Koblentz asked me to continue to teach an Aramaic class after the capstone is completed, to which I have agreed.

This Aramaic workshop will also feature slides from a PowerPoint presentation. Slides will be used to show the similarities and differences between the Semitic languages of Aramaic, Hebrew, and Arabic. Also, slides differentiating between Jewish, Mandaic, Western, and Eastern Aramaic will be presented. Finally, we will view slides containing the Eastern Aramaic alphabet.

Time will be allocated to the participants, after introducing the history and uniqueness of Eastern Aramaic, to pair together and share feedback between themselves on their thoughts about what they have learned. Aramaic's history ties into people's lives in unique ways. It is hoped that the sharing time allows workshop participants to process ideas learned about Aramaic and to be prepared to learn more. Participants in the Aramaic workshop will be encouraged to have a writing utensil and writing journal. Students can also write directly in their copies of *Read and Write*.

A second opportunity for participants to exchange ideas will occur after we review the Chaldean Aramaic alphabet and share strategies to sustain the Aramaic language. Workshop participants will be encouraged to form small groups and share amongst themselves what they have learned. After sharing amongst themselves, participants will be encouraged to share ideas with the group at large.

Figure 1: Aramaic Language Lecture Invitation

## Project Measurements

How does one measure the ripple effects of a pebble tossed into a smooth lake? Teaching an Aramaic course is like that pebble tossed upon the smooth surface of thought. Although there may be immediate growth, the long-term effects of the ripples can be difficult to measure.

Members of SDIMA, Seaside Center for Spiritual Living in Encinitas, and the general public will be invited to the Aramaic workshop. Those who attended a talk I shared on the Aramaic version of the Lord's Prayer at the Encinitas Center for Spiritual Living in July of 2019 will also be invited. There is no charge for this Aramaic workshop. It is hoped that we will be able to post flyers, invite by email, and post ads on Facebook to promote the workshop. The location for the workshop will be the Seaside Center for Spiritual Living in Encinitas, California.

In order to measure the immediate effects of the course, a quantitative survey was created to measure students understanding of the class objective and learning outcomes of the course. Workshop participants will take a pre and post-survey to measure participants' understanding of Aramaic. The purpose of the pre-test is to establish a baseline to show growth after the post-test. This pre-test is a safeguard to prevent error in the data analysis (E. Aguilar, personal communication, Jan. 24, 2020).

| Pre-Survey for Chaldean Aramaic Workshop |
| --- |
| **(1) I am aware of regions in the United States where Chaldean Aramaic is spoken.** |
| 1-Strongly Disagree   2-Disagree   3-Neutral   4-Agree   5-Strongly Agree |
| **(2) I understand that Chaldean Aramaic is near extinction.** |
| 1-Strongly Disagree   2-Disagree   3-Neutral   4-Agree   5-Strongly Agree |

| |
|---|
| **(3) I am familiar with what biblical figures spoke Aramaic.** |
| 1-Strongly Disagree    2-Disagree    3-Neutral    4-Agree    5-Strongly Agree |
| **(4) I understand the similarities and differences between Semitic languages.** |
| 1-Strongly Disagree    2-Disagree    3-Neutral    4-Agree    5-Strongly Agree |
| **(5) I am aware of the different Aramaic dialects.** |
| 1-Strongly Disagree    2-Disagree    3-Neutral    4-Agree    5-Strongly Agree |
| **(6) I am familiar with the Chaldean Aramaic alphabet.** |
| 1-Strongly Disagree    2-Disagree    3-Neutral    4-Agree    5-Strongly Agree |
| Figure 2: Pre-Survey of Aramaic Knowledge |

Participants are asked to rate their responses on a Likert scale from 1 to 5, according to the following order: 1-Strongly Disagree    2-Disagree    3-Neutral    4-Agree    5-Strongly Agree. The Likert scale was chosen because it is the most widely used approach to scaling responses in survey research and often used interchangeably with the term, "rating scale" (Wikipedia, n.d.). Dr. Burton also pointed out that Likert scales are simple for participants to fill out (K. Burton, personal communication, Feb. 3, 2020).

The post-survey adds to the pre-survey, by adding a retrospective clause at the beginning of each question. The post-survey also contained an additional, comprehensive seventh question asking workshop participants to reflect on their understanding of the importance of the preservation of the Aramaic language. Similar to the pre-survey, the post-survey also uses a 5-

point Likert scale. At the end of the post-survey, there is a comment section for participants. The

comment section will be the basis for the qualitative analysis.

| Post-Survey for Chaldean Aramaic Workshop |
|---|
| **(1) After completing the Aramaic workshop, I am aware of regions in the United States where Chaldean Aramaic is spoken.** |
| 1-Strongly Disagree     2-Disagree     3-Neutral     4-Agree     5-Strongly Agree |
| **(2) After completing the Aramaic workshop, I understand that Chaldean Aramaic is near extinction.** |
| 1-Strongly Disagree     2-Disagree     3-Neutral     4-Agree     5-Strongly Agree |
| **(3) After completing the Aramaic workshop, I am familiar with what biblical figures spoke Aramaic.** |
| 1-Strongly Disagree     2-Disagree     3-Neutral     4-Agree     5-Strongly Agree |
| **(4) After completing the Aramaic workshop, I understand the similarities and differences between Semitic languages.** |
| 1-Strongly Disagree     2-Disagree     3-Neutral     4-Agree     5-Strongly Agree |
| **(5) After completing the Aramaic workshop, I am aware of the different Aramaic dialects.** |
| 1-Strongly Disagree     2-Disagree     3-Neutral     4-Agree     5-Strongly Agree |
| **(6) After completing the Aramaic workshop, I am familiar with the Chaldean Aramaic alphabet.** |
| 1-Strongly Disagree     2-Disagree     3-Neutral     4-Agree     5-Strongly Agree |
| **(7) After completing the Aramaic workshop, I understand why Chaldean Aramaic is an important language to preserve.** |
| 1-Strongly Disagree     2-Disagree     3-Neutral     4-Agree     5-Strongly Agree |

Add written comment to final question:

Figure 3: Post-Survey of Aramaic Knowledge

The results of the surveys will be gathered by myself and reviewed following the workshop. Data from the surveys will be used to show whether or not participants increased in their understanding on the importance of the preservation of the Aramaic language. An increase or decrease in response on the Likert scale will be used to measure the progress of the participants and success of the capstone project.

In chapter 4, I will detail how teaching the course on Aramaic actually went. I will use the results of the quantitative surveys, and the change in the Likert score, to substantiate the students learning. I will also reveal the qualitative data analysis from participant feedback. At this point, I will also be able to describe more about the participants.

## CHAPTER 4: Measurements, Results, and Interpretations

**Actions Taken**

The cornerstone of my Capstone Project hinged on the teaching of an Aramaic workshop called, "Preserving Eastern Aramaic." This class took place at the Seaside Center for Spiritual Living in Encinitas, California, on Friday, February 28, 2020, from 7-8 p.m. Each participant's understanding of the Aramaic language was measured through surveys in the following six areas: 1) Geographic locations where Eastern Aramaic is currently spoken in the United States. 2) The urgent need to preserve Eastern Aramaic. 3) Relevance to the Holy Bible and the biblical figures who spoke Aramaic. 4) The connection between Aramaic and the other Semitic languages of Akkadian, Hebrew, Arabic, and Ethiopic. 5) Awareness of the differences between the Eastern Aramaic dialects and Western, Jewish, and Mandaic dialects. 6) Familiarity with the Eastern Aramaic alphabet. A seventh question asked only on the post-survey measured comprehension on the topic of the Preservation of Eastern Aramaic.

Each attendee received a welcome packet that contained a pre and post-survey, an outline of the hour-long course, and a flier promoting Aramaic language books for sale produced by my company, Let in the Light Publishing. A complimentary children's book we produced on learning Aramaic, *Read and Write (R&W),* was included in the welcome packet. At the greeting table, we also had various books produced by Let in the Light on the Aramaic language and culture of Eastern Aramaic speaking people for sale. A clipboard with a sign-up sheet for those wanting to receive a copy of the slide presentation, final capstone project, or company newsletter was also placed on the entry table.

Participants arriving at the talk were greeted at the welcoming table by myself and Rev. Karen Koblentz, the current chair of the San Diego Interfaith Ministerial Association (SDIMA) and outreach minister for the Seaside Center for Spiritual Living. Participants were given a clipboard with a pen, the welcome packet, and directed to a seat in the auditorium. The video screen illuminated the first slide of the presentation which introduced the topic, a brief biography of myself, directions on filling out the pre-survey, and a note thanking them for attending.

Although this talk was on a language, as we were in a place of worship promoting interfaith, we started the meeting with a minute of silent prayer. The presentation had 76 slides. After covering my personal journey into Aramaic, we traced the history and written usage of the Aramaic language over the last four thousand years, from the code of Hammurabi to modern Soureth (spoken Aramaic). We compared the word for peace in Semitic languages and the different scripts of spoken Aramaic today. Then, I conducted a paired-partner exercise and we shared ideas and processed information with each other Afterwards, key information on what we had learned so far was shared with the group.

Next, we reviewed each of the 22 letters of the Eastern Aramaic alphabet. We discussed what each letter's heritage in cuneiform was before the letter became the symbol in the alphabet as outlined by Bazzi and Errico (2015). For example, the symbol for the second letter in the Aramaic alphabet, Beth, signified a house. We also briefly discussed the seven vowels and eleven sounds used in spoken Eastern Aramaic today. One participant volunteered to read the sentence from page three of *Read and Write (2017)*, "A heart filled with love for St. Peter the apostle" in modern Aramaic so participants could hear how the spoken language sounded. This example also proved that it was possible for a non-native speaker to learn and speak Eastern Aramaic.

Our final exercise was to cover sustainability strategies for Eastern Aramaic. These included the following six strategies:

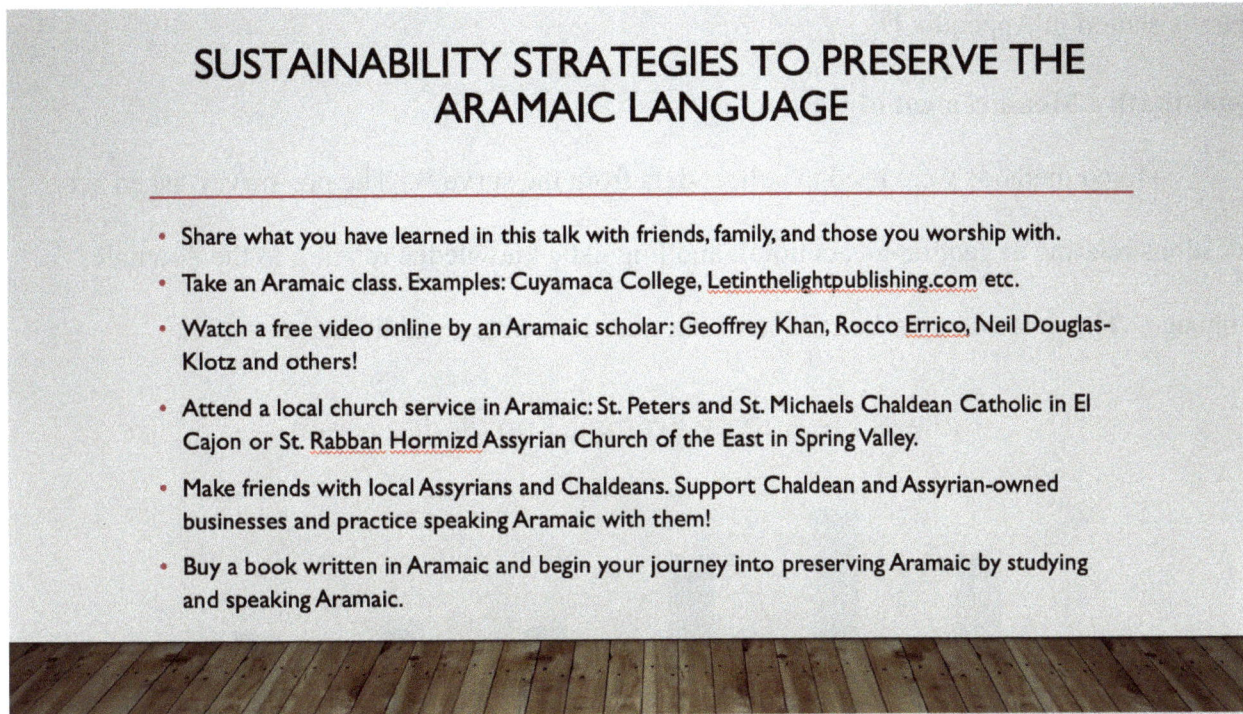

Figure 4: Sustainability Strategies

Participants were then encouraged to share ideas between themselves for a few minutes and share ideas on what they could each to do to preserve Eastern Aramaic. Participants were also encouraged to complete the post-survey. Although three people left immediately at 8 pm, the rest of the group stayed and shared ideas and asked questions. This sharing lasted for two additional hours.

Fortunately, the workshop went smoothly as planned. This was due largely in part to the relationships already built through the talk I gave at Seaside Center for Spiritual Living in July, 2019, on the Aramaic version of the Lord's Prayer. Since 2019, further preparation for the Aramaic workshop through additional Claremont Lincoln University classes and the Capstone Lab enabled this workshop to be scheduled, organized, and implemented within a three-week time period. An example of the slide presentation is shared in Appendix A and an outline of the class is shared in Appendix D.

**Quantitative Measurement of Data**

Mixed methods were used to collect data from the surveys. The pre-survey asked six questions relating to geographic, cultural, and linguistic knowledge relating to the Aramaic language. The post-survey asked the same six questions plus an additional question.

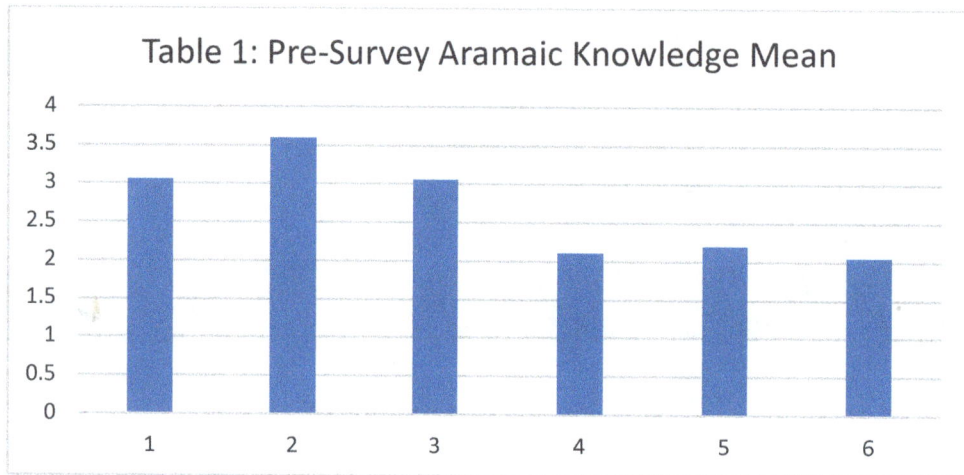

Table 1: Pre-Survey Aramaic Knowledge Mean

The cumulative pre-survey mean was 2.68

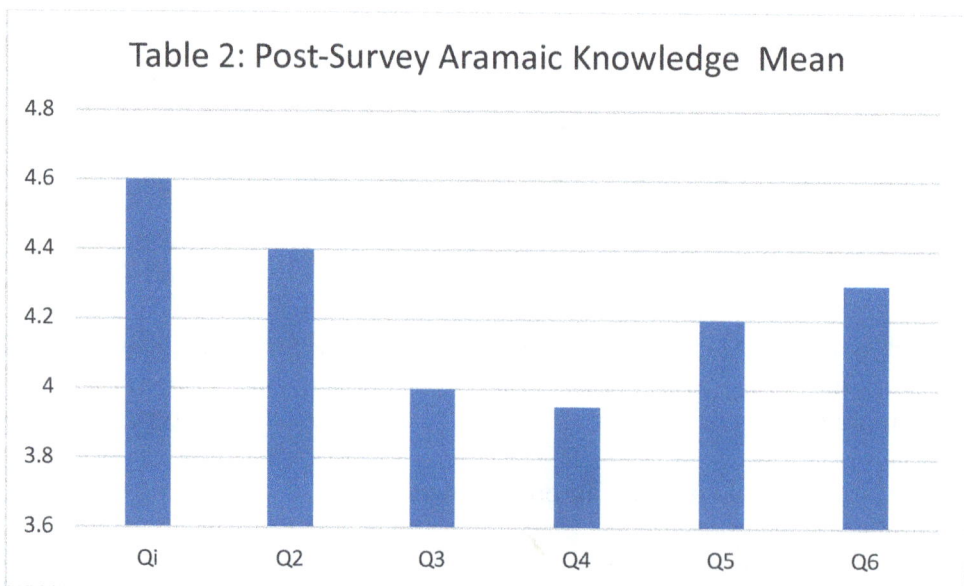

Table 2: Post-Survey Aramaic Knowledge Mean

The cumulative post-survey mean was 4.23

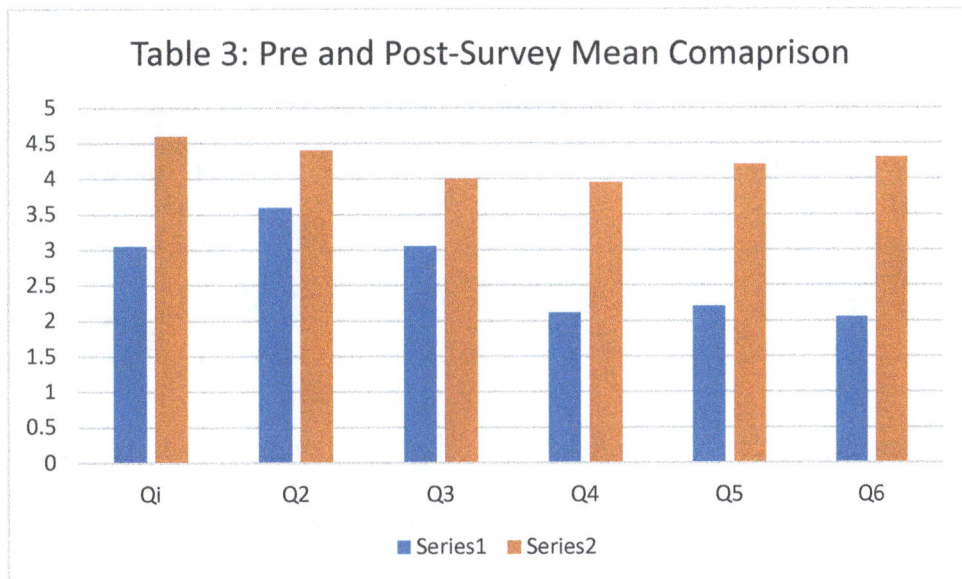

Table 3: Pre and Post-Survey Mean Comaprison

The mean increased from 2.68 to 4.23 for a net gain of 1.55, or 63%.

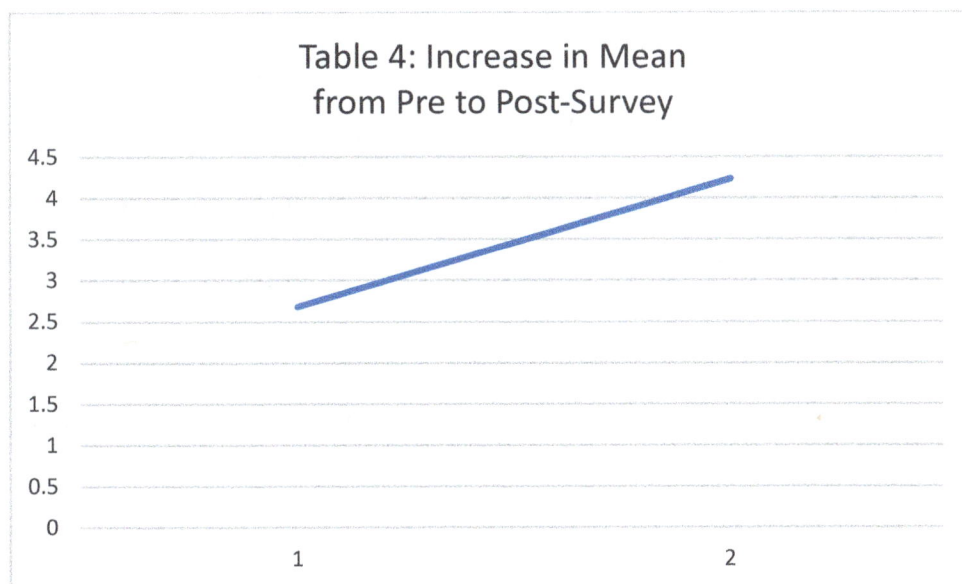

Table 4: Increase in Mean from Pre to Post-Survey

Table 5: Final Gauge of Understaning on Preserving Eastern Aramaic

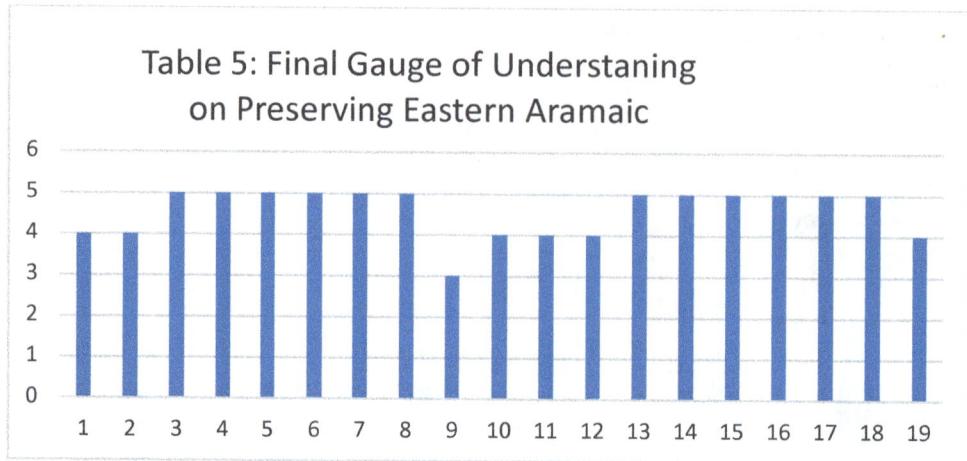

The post-survey contained a cumulative comprehension question on participants' final understanding on the need to preserve the Eastern Aramaic language. The response from the twenty participants averaged 4.58 out of a possible 5. The data used to create these graphs can be found in Appendix B.

**Qualitative Measurement of Data**

The seventh question also had a comment section for reflections from participants. These reflections on the presentation formed the basis of the qualitative analysis. Reflective statements from the participants were organized into three main themes: 1) Preserve a language, preserve an entire culture with a subtheme of using modern technology to achieve this outcome. 2) The relevance of Aramaic to gaining a deeper understanding of Scripture. 3) Affirmations that teaching Aramaic is an effective way to preserve the language.

There were six total comments on the interconnectedness between preserving a language and preserving a culture. Examples include:

- "A language preserves a whole culture."
- "Preserving a language means preserving a culture. The Arabs in El Cajon are preserving their culture through their Chaldean language."

There were two suggestions shared on how to use modern technology to preserve Aramaic:

- "To preserve the language, it would be great if speakers could be recorded speaking or reading books."

- "Perhaps you could film a documentary about 'Aramaic in America,' using the American speakers in San Diego as the focus."

Five attendees commented on the relevance of Aramaic to Scripture. Examples include:

- "My thought is that since the Bible is probably the 'most read' book in Christian societies if the speakers and writers spoke this language, it would be a tragedy to lose this language which could be a conduit to the, 'word of God.'"

- "To understand exactly what Jesus taught."

- "I now understand that Jesus spoke Aramaic. Peter went West (Greek) and Thomas went East (Aramaic)."

The final central theme among participants was that teaching Aramaic was an effective method in preserving the language. Two of the three examples on this theme are:

- "Wonderful presentation!! So informative – has increased my interest in this language! I love the contributions to our world! A humanitarian gift/gifts! I feel I/we owe so much to language, I can't even imagine how our world would have been without. Thanks, Roy."

- "Very informative, interesting, and engaging talk. I've studied modern Aramaic and classical Aramaic some and I still learned a lot. Fr. Bazzi, Prof. Errico, and Roy Gessford have made the ability to learn how to read and write the Chaldean dialect accessible to anyone interested in doing so."

Fourteen of the twenty participants wrote reflections. The comments were all supportive of the effort to preserve the Aramaic language. It is difficult to know why six participate did not leave comments. For a full list of the reflections, please see Appendix C.

**Data Interpretation and Summations**

The first key factor that needed to be determined about the data collected in the surveys was to determine if the pre and post-surveys I created myself were reliable and valid. In order to determine this, I worked with CLU Professor Dr. Ashley Gimbal and the SPSS computer program. First, we ran a Cronbach's alpha test. The results showed that the pre-survey scored a .855 and the post-survey scored a .876. A score over .5 is considered reliable and consistent for a survey, so both the pre and the post-survey for the Preserving Aramaic workshop passed the test.

Next, Dr. Gimbal and I used SPSS to check data points with a paired samples T-test. This test compared the mean increase from 2.68 on the pre-survey to 4.23 on the post-survey. This 63% increase from pre to post-survey is a strong indication of student learning during the hour-long presentation.

Finally, we ran a test to determine P value significance. This test result needed to be less than .05 to be considered significant. The Preserving Aramaic surveys scored .000, which showed strong significance.

The final, seventh comprehensive question gauged students understand in the need for preserving the Aramaic language. Although there were 21 people present, one has a hired computer technician who did not participate in the surveys. The remaining twenty participants all responded to the seventh question which read, "After completing the Aramaic workshop, I understand why Chaldean Aramaic is an important language to preserve." The average response to this question was 4.58 out of 5. All responses either agreed or strongly agreed with the statement, except for one individual, who marked neutral for all responses on the pre and post-survey.

The qualitative data analysis revealed equally strong support for the cause of preserving Eastern Aramaic. The first theme that respondents commented on, "preserving a language helps to preserve a culture," demonstrated to me that participants now understood the larger picture of the contributions of Aramaic speaking populations to humanity. In the lecture we covered how the first cities in recorded history were from Aramaic speaking people. These early city dwellers' contributions to humanity included areas such as mathematics, science, astronomy, music, agriculture, law codes, governance, and many other areas of life. The two suggestions regarding the use of modern technology to support the preservation of culture are indicative to me that students had rapidly processed the information presented and were now able to add valuable suggestions.

Theme number two related to Aramaic's "importance to understanding Scripture." To me this theme corroborated that each person in an interfaith group could find relevance to the Aramaic language for use on their own spiritual journey. Since Aramaic predates Hebrew and Arabic, those that study sacred texts in all three languages should benefit from an increased understanding of Aramaic especially in regard to word origins. The specific comments regarding Jesus speaking Aramaic are relevant because it goes against the current of thought of Western clergy members who preach that Jesus spoke Greek.

The third theme of "teaching Aramaic is an effective solution to preserving the language" indicated that participants had grasped the basics of the Aramaic language and were inspired to practice what they had learned. This theme affirmed what scholars such as Nahir (1988) postulated as the possibility of restoring a language. This third theme of preserving Aramaic through teaching goes against the transformation concept of scholars such as Fishman (1987). In my estimation, the unique spiritual and historical foundation of the Aramaic language are what would allow Aramaic to be restored.

I consider the participants in the workshop essential stakeholders. Each person brought a unique viewpoint. A wide spectrum of individuals were invited. The email list from SDIMA included over 200 members, mostly from the Abrahamic traditions, but also including Buddhist, Daoist, Self-Realization Fellowship (SRF), and New Thought. A Facebook ad was taken out that reached 1,100 people. The criteria for the Facebook ad included female, religious, persecuted, literate, and able to purchase a book.

There were 21 attendees from a variety of backgrounds. Sixteen women and five men were present. I intentionally decided beforehand that due to the sensitive process of learning a language, that I would not conduct a written demographic survey of the participants. From our previous experience with attendees, Rev. Koblentz and I determined that the following faith traditions could be identified among participants: Jewish, Jehovah's Witness, Church of Latter-Day Saints, Church of Religious Science, and Christian Science. There were five people's denominations who were undetermined. The majority of attendees appeared to be in the 50+ age range. At the end of the presentation three copies of *Who are the Chaldeans?* and one copy of *Classical Aramaic I* were purchased.

In Chapter 5, I will provide a project summary, reflection, and conclusion. I will share my highs, lows, and lessons learned as a researcher. I will conclude by providing suggestions and recommendations to follow for future researchers who would like to build on this capstone project.

## CHAPTER 5: Reflections and Recommendations

### Project Summary

Teaching an Aramaic language class to an interfaith group in northern San Diego County served as a positive experiment in preserving the precious Aramaic language. The enthusiasm of the participants who attended the lecture gave me hope for the long-term success of the preservation of Aramaic. At Rev. Koblentz's suggestion, we used a website called Eventbrite to allow attendees to register for the event. On the evening of the event we had seven pre-registered attendees. By the start of the lecture at 7 p.m., twenty-one participants had arrived. The congenial atmosphere allowed for participants to relax and absorb the material. With diversity of race, ethnicity, religion, and age present, a variety of perspectives were represented. The workshop was a pleasure to facilitate.

### Project Impact on the Researcher

This capstone action research project was incredibly rewarding on an academic, personal, professional, and spiritual level. By researching previous scholarship on the Aramaic language, I learned that there was a need for action research in the field of preserving Aramaic. Teaching an Aramaic workshop proved the hypothesis that Aramaic could be preserved. By assessing the data from the surveys, I confirmed what the light in student's eyes indicated – that an increased understanding of Aramaic was taking place. By using literature by my company, Let in the Light, I corroborated that our books are useful in learning Aramaic. I also thought of ways to improve our books. Lastly, by teaching an Aramaic class, my understanding of Aramaic increased. I now have a firmer grasp of the significance of Aramaic within history and sacred texts.

**Project Impact on the Stakeholders**

The participants' response to the Aramaic lecture was encouraging. The quantitative data showed a 63% increase of understanding on the topic. Students' responses to the final question of understanding the need to preserve Aramaic was an affirmative 4.58 out of 5. The qualitative data also showed that students were engaged and intrigued by the topic. I had five requests from participants to receive a copy of the slide presentation and an equal number interested in a copy of the final project.

At the SDIMA meeting the Wednesday following the Friday lecture, I brought in three extra copies of *R&W* that remained from the book promotion. I apologized to the group for the short notice on the Preserving Aramaic talk and offered a free copy of *R&W* to anyone interested. All three copies of *R&W* were distributed. One copy went to a representative of the local Episcopal church. Another copy went to a representative from a Christian Science church. The third copy went to a Daoist who teaches a class on spirituality at a local high school. This individual had brought three high school students to the interfaith meeting. Rev. Koblentz suggested that this high school, and even the nearby middle school, would be excellent places for me to give a talk on Aramaic. Rev. Koblentz has also asked me to teach an Aramaic class at Seaside Center for Spiritual Living in the fall. I let Rev. Koblentz know I am happy to share the Aramaic language in all three of these venues.

**Reflections**

According to Varnon-Hughes (2018), "Language can excite and inspire us, and yet also has the capacity to diminish, legislate, and oppress. Is it possible to give up comfort and certainty in hope of greater community and flourishing?" (p.113). My journey into Aramaic, which began by taking an Aramaic class in 2014, has been full of the elements Varnon-Hughes described. Learning to translate the gospels from Aramaic into English has been one of the highlights of my life. Learning about how native Aramaic speakers were persecuted by ISIS and other government entities for speaking and teaching Aramaic in Iraq and surrounding countries was alarming. As a teacher and promoter of Aramaic, I have witnessed first-hand that relatively few are willing to give up 'comfort and certainty' for the goal of promoting greater understanding and preserving Aramaic.

I was surprised by the resistance to learn Aramaic prevalent among Western Christian clergy members. I realized that many clergy members learned Greek in seminary and learning a new language presented a new field of study. I have been chagrined to learn that at many seminaries ancient language study is no longer requisite. For example, at the Graduate Theological Union in Berkeley, California, where I studied biblical Hebrew and Koine Greek in 2012-13, potential clergy members can now take Spanish or a marketing class in lieu of ancient language study.

The diaspora in the Near and Middle East of native Aramaic speakers has affected the preservation of Aramaic. There are now more native Aramaic speakers living abroad than in their countries of origin. Faith communities such as the Chaldean Catholic Church that traditionally offered mass in Aramaic, have begun offering mass in English or Arabic as well.

A desire to learn Aramaic among westerners exists, and the void to teach Aramaic is being filled by online tutoring, teachers like Dr. Kahn, Dr. Errico, and Fr. Bazzi, and publishing companies like Let in the Light. Although nascent, the effort to preserve Aramaic in the West is occurring largely outside of religious institutions.

The findings of this capstone project also go against the current of academic researchers such as Benthalia & Davies (1993), who encourage transformation rather than preservation of endangered languages. The unique historical and religious role of Aramaic gives Aramaic a sacredness that separates Aramaic from the thousands of languages facing extinction. Although conducted on a small scale, this project showed that interest in Aramaic is alive. Furthermore, the results of the quantitative and qualitative data prove that the basics of Aramaic are not too obscure nor too difficult to be taught to a sampling of the general religious public.

**Recommendations**

Future researchers should certainly be able to repeat and improve upon the research presented in this capstone project. The internet, which helped spawn my interest in Aramaic through a shared video of Dr. Errico, is increasing in its ability to connect those interested in learning Aramaic with those able to teach and research the Aramaic language. The possibility exists that someday soon, an online Aramaic course could be taught to participants from all over the world.

Future researchers may also be able to include a larger spectrum of faith communities. Although resistance to the growth of Aramaic within some conservative factions of Islam exists, other groups within Islam, for example, Sufi, embrace the Aramaic language. Dr. Neil Douglas-Klotz is a Sufi mystic with a large following who promotes learning Aramaic.

One lesson I learned from hosting this event was to avoid teaching the class on a day sacred to a religion. Due to the compacted schedule of an 8-week term, the only day available at the Seaside Center for Spiritual Living in Encinitas to conduct the workshop was a Friday evening. Although we had one person who identified as Jewish in attendance, we also received an email from a rabbi letting us know that she felt we should not be hosting an interfaith event on the Jewish sabbath. Future researchers may be able to avoid the challenge of scheduling on a sacred day by obtaining the university calendar far in advance of the term and planning accordingly.

Another recommendation I would make to future researchers who use surveys is to staple the participant consent form to the anonymous survey. In an effort to maintain anonymity, I kept the forms separate. This method caused minor challenges later when collating data and identifying whose survey belonged to which person. Eventually, I placed a corresponding number on each release form and survey, but the potential for confusion could have been avoided if I had just stapled the two forms together beforehand.

## Conclusions

Preserving a language from extinction requires a concentrated effort. With the case of Hebrew, the only known language to be revived, the sacred texts of the Jewish religion and those entrusted in preserving that text played a pivotal role. Comparing the Semitic languages of Hebrew and Aramaic, one notes that Aramaic has had a wider role in history than Hebrew, having been the lingua franca of the Near East during three successive Near Eastern kingdoms. Furthermore, sacred texts written in Aramaic such as the Peshitta, the Aramaic scriptures, are still in use by some Eastern Christian churches. As Hebrew was the spoken language of the Jews, so Aramaic is still the spoken language of several tribes currently without a homeland such as the Chaldeans and Assyrians. For these reasons, the impetus to preserve the Aramaic language exists.

A major hurdle in preserving Aramaic brought out in this paper by the literature review was that the prognosis for saving languages is dire. The recommendation from several authors was transformation rather than revival. Another obstacle to preserving Aramaic was the recent, tragic loss of a homeland for native Aramaic speakers. This loss has accelerated the pace of the decline of Aramaic. In addition, there is a paucity of support from Western Christian churches to preserve Aramaic at this time. Thus, the movement to preserve Aramaic is taking place largely through outlying sources such as the diaspora community, academia, private teaching, and online sources.

The results of this capstone project indicate that interest in preserving the Aramaic language is alive and widespread among the interfaith community in San Diego, California. The qualitative data in this project highlights the significance of preserving an entire culture when a language is preserved, the deeper understanding of Scripture that comes with preserving Aramaic, and the affirmation that teaching the language is an effective way to preserve the language. This final point was corroborated by the quantitative data. Students' knowledge of the Aramaic language increased 63% from the pre to post-survey. By the end of the lecture, students averaged a 4.58 out of 5 in understanding the need to preserve the Aramaic language.

In the face of difficult odds, it is hoped that the Aramaic language can be preserved. The immediate fruitage of this capstone beyond the surveys was evident in book sales on Aramaic, being asked to give a similar presentation to a local middle and high school, and being given an opportunity to teach an Aramaic course at the Seaside Center for Spiritual Living. Participants at the workshop were encouraged to share what they learned in the presentation with their various faith communities. Future interfaith researchers can build on this project in numerous ways including larger and more diverse class sizes. Through education on the subject of Aramaic language and culture, humanity can awake to the great need to preserve the irreplaceable Aramaic language.

# References

Bacall, J. (2014). *Chaldeans in Detroit.* Charleston, South Carolina: Arcadia Publishing.

Bazzi, M. (2015). *Tilkepe.* (2nd ed.). San, Diego, CA: Let in the Light Publishing.

Bazzi, M. (2017). *Read and Write Aramaic.* San Diego, CA: Let in the Light Publishing.

Bazzi, M. (2017). *Aramaic language Chaldean dialect.* (2nd ed.). San Diego, CA: Let in the Light Publishing.

Bazzi, M. (2018). *Who are the Chaldeans?* (2nd ed.). San Diego, CA: Let in the Light Publishing.

Bazzi, M. & Errico, R. (2015). (3rd ed.). *Classical Aramaic.* San Diego, CA: Let in the Light Publishing.

Benthalia, A. & Davies, E. (1993). Language revival: Restoration of transformation? *Journal of Multilingual & Multicultural Development,* 14(5), 355-374.

Coghill, E. (2009). Four versions of a Neo-Aramaic children's story. *ARAM Periodical* 21, 251-280. Retrieved from: http://www.divaportal.org/smash/get/diva2:1196887/fulltext01.pdf

Coghill, E. (2018). *The Neo-Aramaic dialect of Telkepe.* Retrieved from: http://www.diva-portal.org/smash/get/diva2:1196887/FULLTEXT01.pdf

Cope, L. & Penfield, S. (2011). 'Applied linguistic needed:' Cross-disciplinary networking for revitalization and education in endangered language contexts. *Language and Education,* 25(4), 267-271.

Davis, W. (2009). *The wayfinders: Why ancient wisdom matters in the modern world* (CBC Massey Lecture). Toronto, ON: House of Anansi Press.

Eddy, M. B. (1876). *Science and health with key to the scriptures*. Boston, MA: Christian Science Publishing Society.

Fishman, J. A. (1987). Language spread and language policy for endangered languages. *Proceedings of the Georgetown University round table on languages and linguistics,*. 1-15.

Golden, D. (2001). "Now, like real Israelis, let's stand up and sing": Teaching the national language to Russian newcomers in Israel. *Anthropology & education quarterly,* 32(1), 52-79.

Hanish, S. (2009). Christians, Yazidis, and Mandaeans in Iraq: A Survival Issue. *Digest of Middle East Studies*, 18(1), 1-16. Retrieved from:

https://s3.amazonaws.com/academia.edu.documents/43686969/contentserver.pdf?respons

e-content-

disposition=inline%3B%20filename%3DChristians_Yazidis_and_Mandaeans_in_Iraq.pd

f&x-amz-algorithm=aws4-hmac-sha256&x-amz-

credential=akiaiwowyygz2y53ul3a%2f20191104%2fus-east-

1%2Fs3%2faws4_request&x-amz-date=20191104t231744z&x-amz-expires=3600&X-

amz-signedheaders=host&X-Amz-

signature=097a887d0870f0817fb264ff9f9f381972a2254d3158d5214040a64cfb315b78

Hannah-Fatuhi, A. (2012). *The untold story of native Iraqis*. Bloomington, IN: Xlibiris Press.

Khan, G. (2018). 3.4 The Neo-Aramaic dialects of northern Iraq. *The Languages and Linguistics of Western Asia: An Areal Perspective*, 6, 305.

McWhorter, J. (2015, September). Where do languages go to die? *The Atlantic*. Retrieved

    from: https://www.theatlantic.com/international/archive/2015/09/aramaic-middle-east-

    language/404434/

Nahir, M. (1988). Language planning and acquisition: The 'great leap' in the Hebrew revival.

    *International Handbook of Bilingualism and Bilingual Education, edited by C. B.*

    *Paulson*, 275-95.

Sabar, A. (2013, February). How to save a dying language. *Smithsonian Magazine*. Retrieved

    from: https://www.smithsonianmag.com/innovation/how-to-save-a-dying-language-

    4143017/

Sabar, Y. (2018, November/December). Saving the Aramaic language of Jesus and the Jews.

    *Biblical Archaeology Review*, 24-29.

Suina, J. (2004, September). Native language teachers in a struggle for language and cultural

    survival. *Anthropology & Education Quarterly*. 35 (3), 281-302.

Testen, D. (1985). "The significance of Aramaic r<*n." *Journal of Near Eastern Studies,* 44(2),

    143-146.

Varnon-Hughes, S. (2018). *Interfaith grit: How uncertainty will save us.* Eugene, OR: Wipf &

    Stock.

Wikipedia, (n.d.). Likert Scale. Retrieved from: https://en.wikipedia.org/wiki/Likert_scale

**Appendix A: Slide Presentation**

# APPENDIX A PRESERVING EASTERN ARAMAIC

BY MASTERS OF INTERFAITH ACTION CANDIDATE ROY GESSFORD

CONTACT: LETINTHELIGHTPUBLISHING@GMAIL.COM (PAGE 1 OF *READ AND WRITE*).

IF YOU WOULD, PLEASE FILL OUT THE CONSENT FORMS – YOUR IDENTITY WILL REMAIN ANONYMOUS. ALSO, PLEASE FILL OUT THE PRE-SURVEY. THE POST-SURVEY WILL BE FILLED OUT AT THE END. THESE FORMS ARE ESSENTIAL TO THE RESEARCH ASPECT OF THIS TALK.

©2020 LET IN THE LIGHT PUBLISHING

MY JOURNEY INTO ARAMAIC

## ASILOMAR BIBLE CONFERENCE

HEBREW TUTOR:
MS. RONI RUBINSTEIN

ATTEND CLASSES ON BIBLICAL HEBREW AND KOINE GREEK

- At the Graduate Theological Union (GTU) in Berkeley, California

ARAMAIC SCHOLAR
DR. ROCCO ERRICO

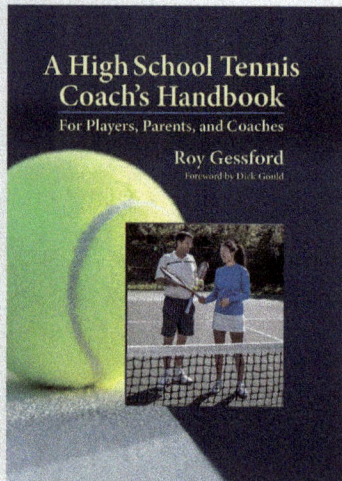

FIRST, WRITE, *A HIGH SCHOOL TENNIS COACH'S HANDBOOK*

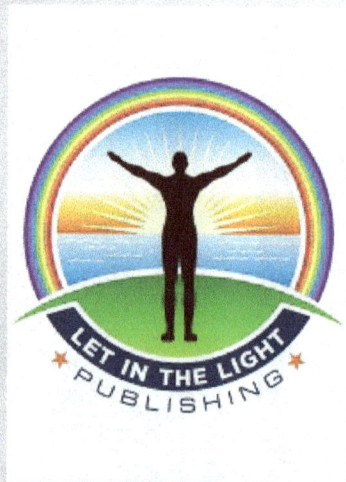

LET IN THE LIGHT PUBLISHING

## SPECIAL VISIT TO SAN DIEGO

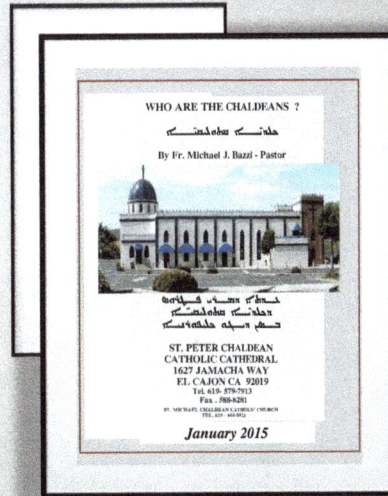

WHO ARE THE CHALDEANS ?

By Fr. Michael J. Bazzi - Pastor

ST. PETER CHALDEAN
CATHOLIC CATHEDRAL
1627 JAMACHA WAY
EL CAJON CA 92019
Tel. 619- 579-7913
Fax . 588-6281

**January 2015**

## MEET WITH FR. MICHAEL BAZZI

# THE HISTORY OF ARAMAIC

## ARAMAIC HAS A LONG AND RICH HISTORY. HAMMURABI'S CODE IS AN EXAMPLE (1750 B.C.E.)

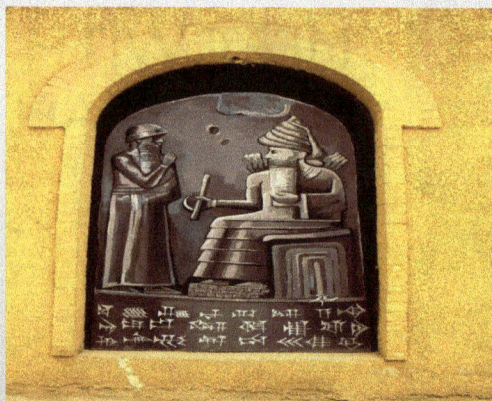

## SUMERIAN AND AKKADIAN ARE EARLY FORMS OF ARAMAIC WHICH USED CUNEIFORM LETTERS

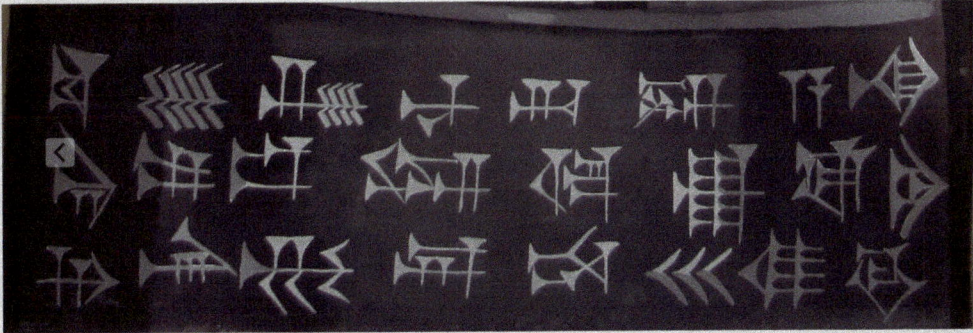

## A HISTORY OF THE EVOLUTION OF ARAMAIC
### (FROM THE INTRODUCTION TO *READ AND WRITE*)

| | |
|---|---|
| Old Aramaic | 925-700 BC |
| Standard Aramaic | 700-200 BC |
| Middle Aramaic | 200 BC-200 AD |
| Late Aramaic | 200 AD-700 AD |

THE NEO-ASSYRIAN
EMPIRE (911-609 B.C.E.)
SPOKE ARAMAIC

THE FIRST QUEEN TO RULE,
SHAMMURAMAT, OR
SAMMU-RAMAT, SEMIRAMIS
(GREEK) SPOKE AN EARLY
FORM OF ARAMAIC
(AKKADIAN)

DURING THE NEO-BABYLONIAN EMPIRE (625-539),
ARAMAIC WAS SPOKEN

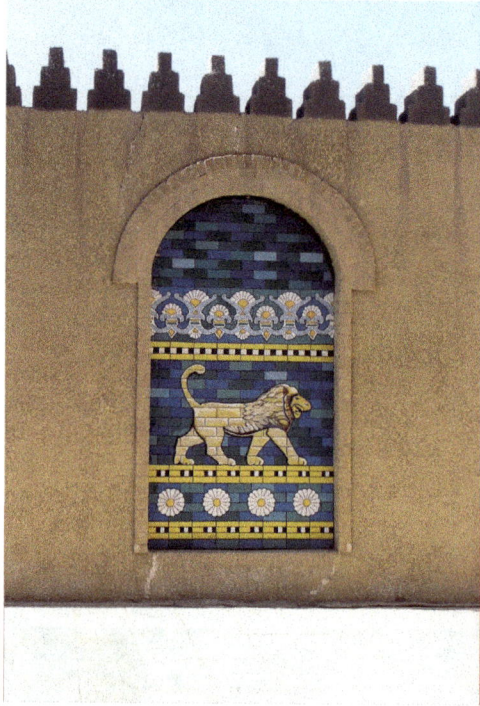

# THE WALLS OF BABYLON

## THE EUPHRATES RIVER

**DURING THE CHALDEAN EMPIRE EARLY ARAMAIC IS RECORDED AS SPOKEN BY:**

- King Nebuchadnezzar and his court
- Portions of the Hebrew scriptures of Daniel, Ezra-Nehemiah
- One verse in the book of Jeremiah (10:11)

# EARLY ARAMAIC WAS SPOKEN IN THE PERSIAN EMPIRE (550-330 B.C.E.)

## THE CYLINDER OF CYRUS THE GREAT IS IN AKKADIAN CUNEIFORM

## AFTER PERSIAN RULE,
## THE DECLINE OF ARAMAIC BEGAN

- The Hellenistic Period saw the rise of Greek (4th century B.C.E.)

- The Roman Empire brought Latin (starting in the 1st century B.C.E.)

- Muslim conquest brought Arabic (Starting in the 7th century A.D. to the present day)

**DURING JESUS' LIFETIME ARAMAIC WAS STILL THE COMMON LANGUAGE OF PALESTINE**

The Lord's Prayer in Estrangela Script in Classical Aramaic

## THE NEW TESTAMENT SCRIPTURES WENT IN TWO DIRECTIONS

WEST WITH THE APOSTLE PETER AND THROUGH THE GREEK LANGUAGE

EAST THROUGH THE APOSTLE THOMAS AND THROUGH ARAMAIC

# KATA

# MAΘΘAION

ܩܘܠܬܐ

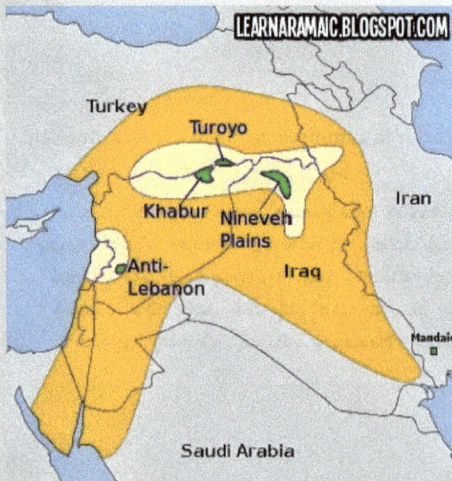

ARAMAIC CONTINUED TO BE SPOKEN IN VARIOUS LOCATIONS

## OVERVIEW OF SEMITIC LANGUAGES

**SEMITIC LANGUAGES:
"SEMITIC" REFERS TO
SHEM, SON OF NOAH,
IN ENGLISH, SAM**

- Akkadian
- Aramaic
- Hebrew
- Arabic
- Ethiopic

## THE WORD FOR PEACE IN ARAMAIC PRONOUNCED "SHLAMA"

ܫܠܡܐ

Note: The four Aramaic letters connect. However, Aramaic has six letters that do not connect (unjoining). The final letter is unjoining.

## SEMITIC LANGUAGES READ FROM RIGHT TO LEFT

THE HEBREW WORD FOR PEACE
PRONOUNCED SHALOM

שלום

Note the spaces between the 4 Hebrew letters
Hebrew block letters are an older Aramaic script

THE ARABIC WORD FOR PEACE
PRONOUNCED SALAAM

سلام

• Note the proximity between the 4 Arabic letters

# OVERVIEW OF DIFFERENT ARAMAIC DIALECTS

ACCORDING TO SCHOLAR GEOFFREY KHAN THERE ARE BETWEEN 100-150 DIFFERENT DIALECTS OF ARAMAIC. SOME ARAMAIC DIALECTS ARE ALREADY EXTINCT.

## THE FOUR MAIN SUBGROUPS OF ARAMAIC DIALECTS ARE:

- Western Aramaic, which includes Jacobite, Meclhite, Galilean, Syriac

- Mandaean Aramaic

- Jewish Aramaic

- Eastern Aramaic also called Assyrian, Neo-Aramaic, or Chaldean Aramaic

## EXAMPLES OF WESTERN ARAMAIC SCRIPTS

SYRIAC

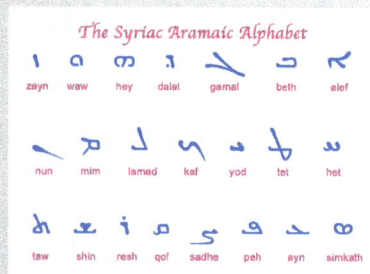

The Syriac Aramaic Alphabet

| zayn | waw | hey | dalat | gamal | beth | elef |
| nun | mim | lamad | kaf | yod | tet | het |
| taw | shin | resh | qof | sadhe | peh | ayn | simkath |

GALILEAN

The Lord's Prayer in Galilean Aramaic

d"-b"-s"mayya'    'abu-nan
who - in - Heaven (is)    Our Father

EXAMPLES OF MANDAIC

NEO-MANDAIC SCRIPT

JAMES MCGRATH'S NEW BOOK, *THE MANDAEAN BOOK OF JOHN*

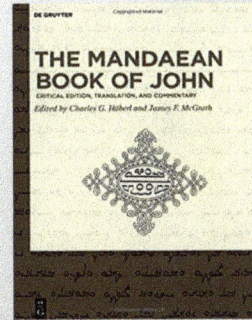

FOR MORE INFO AND PODCASTS VISIT:

WWW.EARLYCHRISTIANTEXTS.COM

## JEWISH ARAMAIC – AN ARAMAIC AND HEBREW SCRIPT USED, FOR EXAMPLE, IN THE BABYLONIAN TALMUD

## EASTERN OR NEO ARAMAIC SCRIPTS FOUND ON PAGE 2 OF *READ AND WRITE*

## KNOWING THE ENGLISH EQUIVALENTS IS HELPFUL – FOUND ON PAGE 4 OF *READ AND WRITE*

**4th : The 26 English alphabet, with the equivalent Aramaic alphabet and sounds**

| A | ܐ | B | ܒ | C | ܟ | D | ܕ | E | ܗ | F-sound | ܦ | G | ܓ |
|---|---|---|---|---|---|---|---|---|---|---|---|---|---|
| H | ܚ | I | ܝ | J-sound | ܔ | K | ܟ | L | ܠ | M | ܡ | N | ܢ |
| O-vowel | ܘ | P | ܦ | Q | ܩ | R | ܪ | S | ܣ | T | ܬ | U-vowel | ܘ |
| V-sound | ܦ | W | ܘ | X | ܟ | Y | ܝ | Z | ܙ | | | | |

## THE CURRENT DIASPORA HAS RELOCATED ARAMAIC SPEAKERS ALL OVER THE WORLD. WITHOUT A HOMELAND, PRESERVING ARAMAIC HAS BECOME EVEN MORE CHALLENGING.

Aramaic speakers emigrated to the United States through Canada around 1900. In the Eastern part of the United States, Aramaic speakers are concentrated in Detroit, Chicago, Green Bay, and New Jersey.

The Western United States has concentrations of Aramaic speakers in San Diego, Los Angeles, San Jose, and Scottsdale, Arizona.

PLEASE PAIR UP AND TAKE A 1-2 MINUTES TO
SHARE IDEAS ABOUT YOUR IMPRESSIONS SO FAR

THE EASTERN ARAMAIC ALPHABET
CONTAINS 22 LETTERS

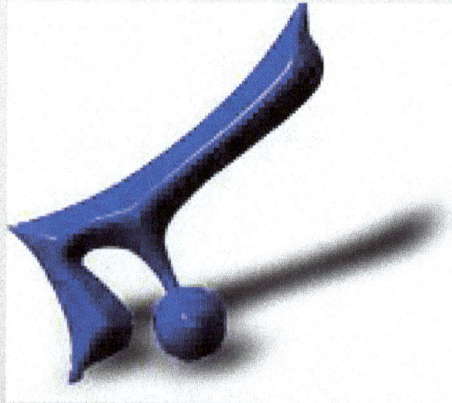

- The Sumerians and Egyptians began their language with pictures (symbols). Later on these symbols were developed into an alphabet. The ancient Assyrians shaped their alphabet from objects and things. The following is a very short summation showing how the Estrangela and Aramaic letters were derived. (*Classical Aramaic*, p. 56-57).

SIX LETTERS, SUCH AS THE FIRST LETTER, ALAP, HAVE A MODERN AND OLDER (ESTRANGELA) FORM

ESTRANGELA ALAP *(PAGE 10*, R&W)

NEO-ARAMAIC ALAP (PAGE 4, R&W)

## THE EARLY ORIGINS OF ALAP FROM CUNEIFORM

- Alap, the first letter of the Aramaic alphabet, was shaped like an ox head, the God of Mesopotamia.

ܒ — THE SECOND LETTER - BETH

- Beth was shaped like an ancient house. (Bayta - ܒܲܝܬܵܐ , house).

THE THIRD LETTER IS CALLED GAMAL - ܓ

ܓ -Gamal resembled a Camel's saddle. (Gamla - ܓܰܡܠܐ , Camel, in English, a camel's hump).

THE FOURTH LETTER, DALATH, HAS TWO FORMS. DALATH RESEMBLED A FIELD AT THE MOUTH OF A RIVER, ALSO DELTA OR TRIANGLE.

ESTRANGELA DALETH

NEO-ARAMAIC OR MODERN DALETH

ܕ

ܕ

ܗ - HE OR HEH, THE FIFTH LETTER, ALSO HAS TWO FORMS. HEH RESEMBLED A TRAP, OR A PIT. (HAUTA - ܚܘܬܐ, A DITCH)

---

**HEH IN ESTRANGELA**                    **HEH IN MODERN SCRIPT**

ܗ                                         ܗ

---

WAW, OR WOW, IS THE SIXTH LETTER. ܘ

---

ܘ Waw resembled the shape of a flower which was

opening. (Warda - ܘܪܕܐ - Flower)

❾ ZAYN, OR ZAIN, IS THE SEVENTH LETTER

❾Zain resembled the head of a weapon – an arrow or a spear. ( Zayna - ܙܲܝܢܵܐ - Weapon)

ܚ HETH IS THE EIGHTH LETTER OF THE EASTERN NEO-ARAMAIC ALPHABET

ܚ Heth resembled a snake in motion .

( Hiwya - ܚܷܘܝܵܐ - Snake)

## TETH IS THE NINTH LETTER

ܛ     Teth resembled a bird

( Tayra - ܛܲܝܪܵܐ - Bird)

## THE TENTH LETTER, YOD OR YODH, IS THE SMALLEST LETTER IN THE ARAMAIC ALPHABET

ܝ Yodh resembled a half – opened palm of the hand as one who is begging.

(Eedha - ܐܝܼܕ݂ܵܐ - Hand)

KAP, THE ELEVENTH LETTER, USES THREE SYMBOLS. THE

SYMBOL, ⲥⲁ ,OR AT THE END OF A WORD WITH A, ⲥ

ⲥⲁ Kap resembled a fist  -  a closed hand.

LAMAD, OR LAMADH, THE TWELFTH LETTER IS
THE TALLEST LETTER. (SIZE 4 ON PAGE 2 OF *R&W*)

ⲗ Lamadh resembled a jaw bone.

מ MEEM RESEMBLED THE SHAPE OF A POND WITH

WATER IN IT. (MAYA - ܡܲܝ̈ܵܐ - WATER).
MEEM, THE THIRTEENTH LETTER, HAS TWO FORMS.

ESTRANGELA AND FINAL FORM    BEGINNING AND MIDDLE MEEM

ܡܡܡ

ם

THE FOURTEENTH LETTER, NOON, ALSO HAS A

DIFFERENT FINAL FORM: ܢ

· ܠ Noon resembled an axe

( Narga - ܢܵܪܓܵܐ - Axe)

## SIMKATH IS THE FIFTEENTH LETTER, ܣ

ܣ Simkath resembled the moon with a face. The moon was the Goddess of all Mesopotamia.

(Sahra - ܣܹܗܪܵܐ - moon).

## ܥ AE IS THE SIXTEENTH LETTER

Ae resembled a side view of an open eye, especially a human eye.

ܥ

(Ayna - ܥܲܝܢܵܐ - eye).

## PE, ܦ, IS THE SEVENTEENTH LETTER

ܦ Pe resembled the shape of a mouth.

(Pooma - ܦܘܿܡܵܐ - mouth;

Poqa - ܦܲܩܵܐ - nose).

## SADE, OR SADHE, IS THE EIGHTEENTH LETTER- ܨ

- ܨ Sadhe resembled a statue.

- (Salma - ܨܲܠܡܵܐ - idol/statue/face).

## QOP IS THE NINETEENTH LETTER - ◻

◻   Qop resembled resembled an

ancient basket made of reeds.

(Qopa – ܩܘܦܐ - basket).

## THE TWENTIETH LETTER, RESH, HAS A MODERN, OR NEO-ARAMAIC, AND AN ESTRANGLEA SYMBOL

**ESTRANGELA**

Resh resembled the human head with a small curl of hair.

(Resha - ܪܝܫܐ - Head).

**NEO-ARAMAIC**

ܪ

ܪ

## THE TWENTY-FIRST LETTER IS SHEEN

Sheen resembled an ancient eastern lamp.

(Shragha — ܫܪܵܓ݂ܵܐ - lamp).

THE FINAL LETTER, TAW, HAS A MODERN AND AN ESTRANGELA SYMBOL.

TAW IN ESTRANGELA        TAW IN MODERN, OR NEO-ARAMAIC

Taw resembled a jar.

(Talma - ܛܲܠܡܵܐ - jar).

# VOCALIZATION MARKS (VOWELS)

## MODERN CHALDEAN ARAMAIC HAS 7 VOWELS
## SEE PAGE 3 OF *READ AND WRITE*

**5th: The seven Aramaic vowels ܩ̈ܢܝܬܐ : ܫܲܒ݂ܥܵܐ : ܙܵܘܥܹ̈ܐ**

| | | |
|---|---|---|
| 1 | SQAPA- ܘܫܦܐ ◌ܷ | Long A= Aa ܐܵ example: ܡܵܪܐ–(Mara) Lord |
| 2 | PTHAHA – ܦܬ݂ܵܚܐ ◌ܲ | Short A= Ah ܐܲ example: ܡܲܠܟܵܐ–(Malka) King |
| 3 | ZLAMA PSHEEQA- ܙܠܵܡܵܐ ܦܫܝܩܐ ◌ܷ | Short I= I ܐܝܼ example: ܡܝܼܫܚܐ–(Mishha) Oil |
| 4 | ZLAMA QASHYA- ܙܠܵܡܵܐ ܩܵܫܝܐ ◌ܹ | Long E = AY ܐܹ example: ܪܹܫܐ–(Raysha) Head |
| 5 | RWAHA – ܪܘܵܚܐ ܘ | Long O=OH ܘ example: ܦܘܿܩܐ –(Poqa) Nose |
| 6 | RWASA – ܪܘܵܨܐ ܘ | Long U= U ܘ example: ܙܘܿܙܐ –(Zooza) Money |
| 7 | HWASA – ܚܒ݂ܵܨܐ ܝ | Long Y- EE ܝ example: ܡܝܼܟ݂ܵܐܝܠ–(Mikhael) Michael |

## VOWELS IN A SENTENCE

| Long Y | Long O | Short A | | Long E | | Long U | | Long A | Short I |

ܝܼܬܼܪ ܗܠܸܝܼ ܣܘܿܬܼܵ ܠܸܕܘܿܗܿܝ ܘܡܿܬܵܝ ܦܝܼܟܵܬܵܘܗ ܥܠܸܝܼܢܵܬ

**(A heart filled with love for St. Peter the Apostle)**

---

## EXTRA: THE NINE SOUNDS IN MODERN ARAMAIC SIX ARE COMMON TO CLASSICAL ARAMAIC (P. 5,7)

- Because of the influence of neighboring languages, six of the 22 letters were modified in sound in classical Aramaic BGaDiKPaT (ܒܓܕܟܦܬ) and were added to the alphabet. However, only four of the six letters (ܒܓܟܬ) were given new sounds while two of them (p ܦ b ܒ) for some unknown reason were pronounced like the letter (ܘ) waw=w(ܘ).

- Of the six modified letters, five were modified simply by adding a dot underneath the letter, and one (ܦ) by merely adding a semi-circle attached below the letter (ܦ).

| | 1 | 2 | 3 | 4 | 5 | 6 | 7 | 8 | 9 |
|---|---|---|---|---|---|---|---|---|---|
| | غ Gh | ذ D | خ KH | ڤ V | ظ Dh | ج J | چ CH | ف F | ث TH |

**ALL NINE MODERN ARAMAIC SOUNDS (P. 5, R&W)**

## SUSTAINABILITY STRATEGIES TO PRESERVE THE ARAMAIC LANGUAGE

- Share what you have learned in this talk with friends, family, and those you worship with.

- Take an Aramaic class. Examples: Cuyamaca College, Letinthelightpublishing.com etc.

- Watch a free video online by an Aramaic scholar: Geoffrey Kahn, Rocco Errico, Neil Douglas-Klotz and others!

- Attend a local church service in Aramaic: St. Peters and St. Michaels Chaldean Catholic in El Cajon or St. Rabban Hormizd Assyrian Church of the East in Spring Valley.

- Make friends with local Assyrians and Chaldeans. Support Chaldean and Assyrian-owned businesses and practice speaking Aramaic with them!

- Buy a book written in Aramaic and begin your journey into preserving Aramaic by studying and speaking Aramaic.

## SUSTAINABILITY STRATEGIES TO PRESERVE THE ARAMAIC LANGUAGE

- Share what you have learned in this talk with friends, family, and those you worship with.

- Take an Aramaic class. Examples: Cuyamaca College, Letinthelightpublishing.com etc.

- Watch a free video online by an Aramaic scholar: Geoffrey Kahn, Rocco Errico, Neil Douglas-Klotz and others!

- Attend a local church service in Aramaic: St. Peters and St. Michaels Chaldean Catholic in El Cajon or St. Rabban Hormizd Assyrian Church of the East in Spring Valley.

- Make friends with local Assyrians and Chaldeans. Support Chaldean and Assyrian-owned businesses and practice speaking Aramaic with them!

- Buy a book written in Aramaic and begin your journey into preserving Aramaic by studying and speaking Aramaic.

## THANK YOU FOR YOUR ATTENDANCE!

- Please fill out your Post-surveys. These surveys are essential to the research. Please leave a comment on Question #7 if you are inclined to do so.

- If you would like a copy of the presentation or a final copy of my capstone action research project, please leave you email on the sign-up sheet or email me at letinthelightpublishing@gmail.com (Page 1 of *Read and Write*). You may also call me with follow-up questions: (619)586-3523.

## Appendix B: Quantitative Survey

| Appendix B | | | | | | |
|---|---|---|---|---|---|---|
| Preserving Aramaic Pre-Survey | | | | | | |
| | Q1 | Q2 | Q3 | Q4 | Q5 | Q6 |
| Participant 1 | 4 | 5 | 4 | 2 | 2 | 4 |
| Participant 2 | 4 | 4 | 3 | 3 | 2 | 4 |
| Participant 3 | 4 | 4 | 3 | 3 | 3 | 3 |
| Participant 4 | 1 | 4 | 1 | 1 | 1 | 1 |
| Participant 5 | 3 | 4 | 3 | 1 | 1 | 2 |
| Participant 6 | 5 | 3 | 4 | 1 | 1 | 1 |
| Participant 7 | 1 | 1 | 1 | 1 | 1 | 1 |
| Participant 8 | 1 | 4 | 2 | 1 | 1 | 1 |
| Participant 9 | 1 | 2 | 3 | 1 | 1 | 1 |
| Participant 10 | 3 | 3 | 3 | 3 | 3 | 3 |
| Participant 11 | 1 | 3 | 2 | 1 | 1 | 1 |
| Participant 12 | 4 | 3 | 4 | 2 | 1 | 1 |
| Participant 13 | 4 | 4 | 3 | 3 | 3 | 2 |
| Participant 14 | 4 | 5 | 4 | 4 | 4 | 1 |
| Participant 15 | 5 | 3 | 3 | 3 | 4 | 3 |
| Participant 16 | 1 | 4 | 4 | 3 | 2 | 1 |
| Participant 17 | 5 | 5 | 4 | 4 | 4 | 5 |
| Participant 18 | 4 | 4 | 4 | 1 | 2 | 2 |
| Participant 19 | 3 | 4 | 3 | 2 | 4 | 1 |
| Participant 20 | 3 | 3 | 3 | 3 | 3 | 3 |
| Total | 61 | 72 | 61 | 43 | 44 | 41 |
| Mean | 3.05 | 3.6 | 3.05 | 2.15 | 2.2 | 2.05 |

| | | Mean-Pre | Mean-Post | | Change in Mean | |
|---|---|---|---|---|---|---|
| | Qi | 3.05 | 4.6 | | Pre | 2.68 |
| | Q2 | 3.6 | 4.4 | | Post | 4.23 |
| | Q3 | 3.05 | 4 | | Diff. | 1.55 |
| | Q4 | 2.15 | 3.95 | | | |
| | Q5 | 2.2 | 4.2 | | | |
| | Q6 | 2.05 | 4.3 | | | |
| Total | | 16.1 | | | | |
| Mean | | 2.68333333 | | | | |

PRESERVING ARAMAIC

| Appendix B | | | | | | | |
|---|---|---|---|---|---|---|---|
| **Preserving Aramaic Post-Survey** | | | | | | | |
| | Post Q1 | Post Q2 | Post Q3 | Post Q4 | Post Q5 | Post Q6 | Post Q7 |
| Participant 1 | 4 | 4 | 4 | 4 | 4 | 2 | 4 |
| Participant 2 | 5 | 5 | 5 | 4 | 4 | 4 | 4 |
| Participant 3 | 4 | 4 | 3 | 4 | 4 | 4 | 4 |
| Participant 4 | 5 | 5 | 5 | 4 | 5 | 5 | 5 |
| Participant 5 | 5 | 4 | 4 | 4 | 4 | 4 | 5 |
| Participant 6 | 5 | 5 | 4 | 4 | 4 | 5 | 5 |
| Participant 7 | 4 | 4 | 3 | 3 | 3 | 4 | 5 |
| Participant 8 | 5 | 5 | 5 | 4 | 4 | 5 | 5 |
| Participant 9 | 5 | 5 | 4 | 4 | 5 | 5 | 5 |
| Participant 10 | 3 | 3 | 3 | 3 | 3 | 3 | 3 |
| Participant 11 | 5 | 4 | 4 | 4 | 4 | 5 | 4 |
| Participant 12 | 5 | 4 | 4 | 4 | 4 | 4 | 4 |
| Participant 13 | 4 | 4 | 4 | 4 | 4 | 4 | 4 |
| Participant 14 | 5 | 4 | 4 | 4 | 5 | 4 | 5 |
| Participant 15 | 4 | 4 | 4 | 4 | 4 | 4 | 5 |
| Participant 16 | 5 | 5 | 4 | 4 | 4 | 5 | 5 |
| Participant 17 | 5 | 5 | 5 | 5 | 5 | 5 | 5 |
| Participant 18 | 5 | 5 | 4 | 4 | 5 | 5 | 5 |
| Participant 19 | 5 | 5 | 3 | 4 | 5 | 5 | 5 |
| Participant 20 | 4 | 4 | 4 | 4 | 4 | 4 | 4 |
| | 92 | 88 | 80 | 79 | 84 | 86 | 91 |
| | 4.6 | 4.4 | 4 | 3.95 | 4.2 | 4.3 | 4.55 |

| Appendix B | | |
| --- | --- | --- |
| | Question 7 | |
| Participant 1 | 4 | |
| Participant 2 | 4 | |
| Participant 3 | 5 | |
| Participant 4 | 5 | |
| Participant 5 | 5 | |
| Participant 6 | 5 | |
| Participant 7 | 5 | |
| Participant 8 | 5 | |
| Participant 9 | 3 | |
| Participant 10 | 4 | |
| Participant 11 | 4 | |
| Participant 12 | 4 | |
| Participant 13 | 5 | |
| Participant 14 | 5 | |
| Participant 15 | 5 | |
| Participant 16 | 5 | |
| Participant 17 | 5 | |
| Participant 18 | 5 | |
| Participant 19 | 4 | |
| Participant 20 | 87 | |
| Average | 4.57894737 | |

## Appendix C: Qualitative Survey Data

**Survey Reviews from Preserving Aramaic on 2/28/2020**

Participant # 2: " A language preserves a whole culture."

Participant # 3: "Historical value is important."

Participant # 5: "My thought is that since the Bible is probably the "most read" book in Christian societies. If the speakers and writers spoke this language, it would be a tragedy to lose this language which could be a conduit to the, "word of God."

Participant # 6: "Preserving a language means preserving a culture. The Arabs in El Cajon are preserving their culture through their Chaldean language."

Participant # 7: "I now understand that Jesus spoke Aramaic. Peter went West (Greek) and Thomas went East (Aramaic).

Participant #11: "To preserve the language, it would be great if speakers could be recorded speaking or reading books."

Participant # 14: "To understand exactly what Jesus taught."

Participant # 15: "Wonderful presentation!! So informative – has increased my interest in this language! I love the contributions to our world! A humanitarian gift/gifts! I feel I/we owe so much to language, I can't even imagine how our world would have been without. Thanks, Roy."

Participant # 16: "It would be great to have some biblical passages that we feel confused about to be translated in 'Aramaic' just to see how similar it was to the translation."

Participant # 17: "Very informative, interesting, and engaging talk. I've studied modern Aramaic and classical Aramaic some and I still learned a lot. Fr. Bazzi, Prof. Errico, and Roy Gessford have made the ability to learn how to read and write the Chaldean dialect accessible to anyone interested in doing so."

Participant # 18: "Perhaps you could film a documentary about "Aramaic in America," using the American speakers in San Diego as the focus."

Participant # 19: "To understand what Jesus taught, understanding Aramaic seems very important and exciting."

Participant # 20: "Very uneducated on this subject. This is totally new to me."

# Appendix D: Course Outline

**"Preserving the Aramaic Language"**

**San Dieguito Interfaith Ministerial Association**
**Seaside Center for Spiritual Living, Encinitas, California**
**Date: Friday, February 28, 2020**

**Time: 7 :00 pm**
**Duration: One hour**

**Facilitator:**
Roy Gessford, B.A. University of California, San Diego
Founder, Let in the Light Publishing, San Diego, CA
Candidate, Masters of Interfaith Action, Claremont Lincoln University, Claremont, CA

**Workshop Objective**
This workshop will introduce participants to the Aramaic language and the challenges surrounding Aramaic's longevity.

**Workshop Learning Outcomes**
1. Expose participants to the history of Aramaic / Relevance of Aramaic to sacred texts
2. Differentiate between the different types of Aramaic dialects
3. Understand the basics of the Aramaic alphabet
4. Sustainability strategies for the Aramaic language

**Workshop Outline**

Participant Action Release forms

Complete Pre-survey

Intro and Brief History of Aramaic Language (Ancient to modern)

Distinction between Aramaic, Hebrew, and Arabic; distinction between Aramaic dialects (Eastern, Western, and Jewish)

Paired feedback exercise

Introduction to the Chaldean (Eastern) Aramaic alphabet and review sustainability strategies for Aramaic Language

Small group feedback exercise

Complete Post- survey

Conclusion and gratitude

<h2>Appendix E: Participant Release Forms</h2>

2/28/2020

<h3>Participant Information and Consent</h3>

**Invitation**

You are being asked to take part in a research/dialogue project. It will explore the Aramaic language. It is being conducted by Roy Gessford who is studying towards a Masters of Interfaith Action at Claremont Lincoln University.

**What Will Happen**

An Aramaic workshop will be given at Seaside Center for Spiritual Living in conjunction with San Diego Interfaith Ministerial Association (SDIMA). The course will be an hour in length with the goal of introducing participants to the Aramaic language and the challenges surrounding Aramaic's longevity. There will be a pre and post survey to gauge the learning of the workshop participants. Surveys will be used as a measurement tool and names of participants identity will remain anonymous.

**Potential Risks/Benefits**

The benefits of learning Aramaic are increased understanding of scriptural texts, historical documents, and the oldest spoken language by mankind.

Learning a new language definitely gets one outside one's own comfort zone. Risks associated with learning something new apply such as a broadened perspective, increased intelligence and insight, and overcoming fear.

**Time Commitment**

The time commitment will be one hour on a weekday evening.

**Participants' Rights/Confidentiality**

I will give priority to your interests at all times. To protect your interests in my final report, I promise the following:

- Your identity will be protected at all times in my final report unless you give me specific permission to use your name.

- You are free at any time to withdraw from the research project, whereupon I will destroy all data relating to you. I will report that a participant decided to leave the project, and reflect on ways the project might have been more conducive to all participants.

Individuals must be 18 years of age or older to participate.

## Cost, Reimbursement, and Compensation

Your participation in this study is voluntary. You will NOT receive any compensation nor will you be asked to pay fees of any kind.

## Informed Consent Signature Line

By signing below, you agree that: (1) you have read and understood the Participant Information Sheet, (2) questions about your participation in this study have been answered satisfactorily, and (3) you are taking part in this research study voluntarily (without coercion).

Researcher's Name ___Roy Gessford_____
Date_____1/25/2020_____


Participants Name (Printed) _____

Signed _____     Date _____

## Follow Up After Completion of the Project

☐ I would like follow-up on this project. Please email me the final report of the CAP.

☐ Do nothing. I absolve the researchers of any obligation to contact me about this project.

NOTE: If at any time you have any questions or concerns about the project, you may contact the Dean of Capstone Studies at Claremont Lincoln University, Dr Ashley Gimbal. Please contact her by email: agimbal@claremontlincoln.edu, or call the university: 909-667-4400.

www.ingramcontent.com/pod-product-compliance
Lightning Source LLC
Chambersburg PA
CBHW050416110426
42812CB00006BA/1909